LOVE REVOLUTION

CREATING A KINSHIP OF CARE

HOLLY CLARK

PRAISE

"In *Love Revolution: Creating a Kinship of Care,* author Holly Clark takes readers on a captivating journey through the intricate web of relationships that bind together humanity and the more-than-human world. Through tales of compassion, cooperation, and coexistence, readers are invited to reconsider their relationship with the natural world and embrace a deeper understanding of our shared existence. *Love Revolution* is a thought-provoking ode to the beauty of and the interconnectedness of all living beings, inspiring readers to nurture a sense of kinship and reverence for our shared home."

~alix lutnick, Ph.D

"After reading *Love Revolution: Creating a Kinship of Care,* I was reminded of the first lines of Sonnet 43 by Elizabeth Barrett Browning, 'How do I love thee? Let me count the ways.' In this book by Holly Clark, the list is long and rich and deep and wide. I could not help but think that here is what love looks like: words and stories born through lived experience and the intention of an open heart."

~Carolyn Finney, Author *Black Faces, White Spaces: Reimagining the Relationship of African Americans to the Great Outdoors*

"*Love Revolution: Creating a Kinship of Care* is pure poetry. This book is healing to read; savoring it is like receiving the ingredients for a dish that nourishes the soul. The way in which Holly writes, the language and the words, inspires the remembrance of the divinity and connection we all know within. *Love Revolution* inspires us to fully embody that divinity as a gateway to birthing a new world."

~Soul Divine, Director of *It Ain't Pretty*

"People sometimes ask me why I'm so enraptured with my dog, and I've found it hard to articulate the many reasons. Now I can just hand them this book. In *Love Revolution: Creating a Kinship of Care,* author Holly Clark articulates eloquently the deep oneness we feel when we connect with nature and our more-than-human companions. She inspires us through her experiences to expand our consciousness by living in a state of loving awareness and acknowledging the grace that's all around. Holly's soothing words light a trail to the remembrance of our innate goodness, reminding us that by slowing down, listening, and softening, we will find our collective way home. I am in awe of the wisdom contained in these pages; may it serve as a lantern to guide us forward. Thank you, Holly, for living your passion and inspiring us to embrace our individual and universal magnificence."

~Angelyn Rudd

"*Love Revolution: Creating a Kinship of Care* calls us into a state of greater presence, intentionality, and connection through deliberate connection with the natural world and the beings around us. I was inspired by Holly's romantic wonder of the natural realm and deeply moved by the poetic stories of their beloved companions. I felt a clear, gentle, and compelling invitation into delightful embodiment, to revel in this incredible creation of earth. Holly's vision of this world is one I want to invest in."

~Liesl Nayeli, LSCW

"I can hardly think of anyone who could literally create a Love Revolution but Holly Clark. It's a fitting title from one of the most loving people I know. Her love of life, all life, be it plant, animal, or human, is intense and genuine. She beautifully weaves the love of her dogs to the interconnectedness of our existence on this planet. One of the reasons I love dogs is because they keep me present, they remind me to forgive quickly, they inspire play and wonder, and keep me connected to nature. Holly's stories and observations illustrate not only this special bond, but how it can lead to a fulfilling life and improve our relationship to the earth by being better stewards of this one and only planet. Thank you, Holly, for writing this much-needed book."

~Laura Shine, Creator of WFPK's *The Paws Report*

PRAISE

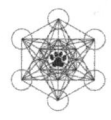

"*Love Revolution* is a poem, a paean, a song, and an outpouring of love and wisdom. It is a doorway to the sacred with the power to transform us individually and collectively. Rumi, the Sufi poet, and Rumi, Holly's beloved dog, join Holly as teachers for all of us who seek a world of peace, joy, and true harmony."

~Zoe Weil, President of The Institute for Humane Education, author of *The Solutionary Way*

"We have so much to learn from our animal companions—if only we open our hearts and minds to their teachings. Holly Clark and her little dog, Rumi—whom I fostered for a local humane society after she was found ill with heartworms and needing a leg amputation to save her life —remind us that by choosing to be more present with ourselves and our 'more-than-human collaborators,' we can find deeper meaning, interconnectedness, joy and boundless love for ourselves and everyone and everything around us."

~Andrea Blair, The Kentucky Humane Society

"*Love Revolution: Creating a Kinship of Care* is a meditation, and a sweet call to presence and right relationship in the world. Her beautiful words soften my heart and I feel myself resting in what she knows, 'to believe ourselves and our world into a healed, whole and radiant state of being.' Love Revolution is both a deep, intimate exploration, and a practical invitation into this "earthly, embodied journey of embracing the beauty of our interconnectedness and the call to action inspired by that awareness."

~Lynn Fraser, Stillpoint

"To walk the beauty way with Holly Clark in Love Revolution: Creating a Kinship of Care, we are invited to awaken to the transformative power of forging and foraging connection and communion with all living beings, heralding a revolutionary shift in consciousness that propels us on the path of perfect love, compassion, and kindness. Holly advocates for and inspires our embracing of a radical understanding of interconnectedness—a recognition that all life forms are inherently linked and deserving of our reverence.

Through vivid prose and insightful anecdotes, she navigates readers on a journey toward a deeper understanding and celebration of this interconnected web of existence. Her invitations and illuminations serve as a timely reminder of the urgent need for humanity to honor the inherent worth and dignity of every living being. By cultivating a mindset of communion, we not only enrich our own lives but also contribute to the creation of a more just, equitable, and harmonious existence for all beings with whom we share this planet. Each page is a pathway to deeper exploration and greater intimacy with the more-than-human world. As we are guided on this journey of awakening, we discover that engaging with this realm can serve as a catalyst for personal and collective transformation. Along the way, accompanied by the love of our three and four-legged companions, we are invited to take pause and allow ourselves to be permeated by the greater possibility of revolutionary devotion and communion with this 'gorgeous web of existence.'

By cultivating a sense of reverence and respect for the natural world, we open ourselves up to a deeper understanding of our place within the larger web of life. And by immersing ourselves intimately in the beauty and intricacies of nature, we are offered glimpses into the deeper mysteries of existence that offer us expansion individually and collectively. Find your harmony in the "universal song of love" and remember why you are here. Sing with the symphony of life, the song that reminds you that we all belong."

~Amy Smiley and Renee Ananda, Troubadours of Divine Bliss

Love Revolution: Creating A Kinship of Care
By Holly Clark

Copyright © 2024 Holly Clark

All rights reserved. No part of this book may be used or reproduced by any means, graphic, electronic, or mechanical, including photocopying, recording, taping, or by any information storage retrieval system without the written permission of the publisher except in the case of brief quotations embodied in critical articles and reviews.

Without limiting the rights under copyright reserved above, no part of this publication may be reproduced, stored in or introduced into a retrieval system, or transmitted in any form or by any means (electronic, mechanical, photocopying, recording, or otherwise), without the prior written permission of both the copyright owner and the above publisher of this book.

Because of the dynamic nature of the Internet, any web addresses or links contained in this book may have changed since publication and may no longer be valid.

The views expressed in this work are solely those of the author and do not necessarily reflect the views of the publisher, and the publisher hereby disclaims any responsibility for them.

Published by Flower of Life Press
www.floweroflifepress.com

Flower of Life Press books may be ordered through booksellers or by contacting: support@floweroflifepress.com

Cover and interior design by Astara Jane Ashley

Library of Congress Control Number: Available upon request.

ISBN: 979-8-9909775-5-6

DEDICATION

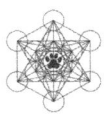

This is dedicated to all the exquisite beings along the path who have inspired a love in my soul so enormous that it had to be shared. To the trees, stones, stars, flowers, raindrops, butterflies, angels, and all other miracles of creation, thank you. I bow to all the brilliant humans who have been reflections of loving kindness on this evolutionary life adventure. I especially honor my beloved ancestors for living and loving so that I could be alive during this incredible time of awakening and remembering. And with all of my heart, I thank the amazing canine soulmates who have walked beside me through every season of life. You've been my anchors, my greatest teachers, my steadiest companions, my truest loves, and my best friends. To Rumi and Basil: You opened me to the vast beauty of true love, which is the greatest blessing I could have ever imagined, and I am eternally grateful. And lastly, this is dedicated to the Beloved, the Divine Creator and Source of all that is, for living and loving through me and connecting us all in a magnificent, ever-evolving tapestry of grace.

While this book opens its arms and heart to celebrate the vast range of miraculous luminaries (plant, animal, mineral, and beyond) who continue to guide me on my journey, it was initially inspired by my incredible relationships with the cats and dogs in my life, all of whom were rescues. Thus, a portion of the proceeds from this book will go toward enhancing the lives of those whose voices often go unheard through supporting the amazing work of the International Humane Society and other collaborating rescue organizations. Support your local shelters, offer a forever home to a sweet being in need, and hug your babies.

TABLE OF CONTENTS

Foreword by Heather Ensworth, Ph.D xi

Introduction 1

    Chapter 1: Love 3

    Chapter 2: Soulmates 17

    Chapter 3: Intention 33

    Chapter 4: Trees 45

    Chapter 5: Winged Ones 57

    Chapter 6: Flowers 69

    Chapter 7: The Cosmos 81

    Chapter 8: Water 93

    Chapter 9: Embodiment 103

    Chapter 10: Ambrosia 119

    Chapter 11: Angels and Ancestors 131

    Chapter 12: Breath 141

    Chapter 13: Presence 155

Invitation 167

Love Revolution Practices 173

Acknowledgments 175

About the Author 177

FOREWORD

By Heather Ensworth, Ph.D

This book is a beautiful love song to the beings who share our world with us—from our dog, cat, and equine companions to beloved trees, plants, other animals and birds, the waters of the Earth, and planetary and star beings in the sky. Holly guides us in how to come back into right relationship with the sacredness of the life around us and how to open to the love that is available to us as we reconnect with the consciousness of the Earth and sky and all of life.

Evolution biologist Elisabet Sahtouris has written in her book *Earthdance: Living Systems in Evolution* that the evolutionary journey of all species is from competition and "survival of the fittest" into maturity and the realization that we actually thrive through interdependence and being in mutual relationship with the life around us. Sadly, we humans have not yet matured into this higher evolutionary state and have caused massive disruption and destruction on the planet in our false sense of superiority and treatment of the life around us as resources to be used and abused rather than as sacred beings to honor and respect. It is time now for us to heal and awaken.

This beautiful book guides us in how we can make that healing shift and come back into balance and not only honor the life around us but realize how much we have to gain by learning from and communing with the conscious and loving animals, plants, and beings who are here with us. Holly helps us understand the practical steps we can take to move into this higher level of consciousness and remembrance of our interconnectedness and how to open to and rediscover the joy of being in relationship with the sacredness of all of the life around us.

INTRODUCTION

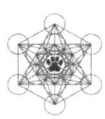

My earliest recollection of reverence is resting barefoot in the grass, marveling at impatiens seed pods bursting forth with an explosion of new life under the gentle squeeze of my chubby, three-year-old fingers. Winky, my best friend and beloved canine companion, was devotedly at my side, and I have a distinct memory of us looking into each other's eyes in wondrous awe. At the same time, I laughed in delight, and he smiled knowingly, deep reverence beaming forth from both of our hearts. I remember the golden warmth of the Sun on my bare legs and the comforting softness of Winky's smooth fur as we savored the sweet magic of the incredible Universe we all call home. In that holy moment, my toddler awareness blossomed open to the sacredness of being alive, and something deep inside me committed to living my life in service to this exquisite, wild blessing.

That reverence is still alive in me today, many Moons later, and it's stronger than ever. I'm in awe of the vast wisdom contained in seed pods, the infinite love we share with our canine companions, the power of sunlight to awaken new codes of consciousness, and the grace of being alive together during this time of radical transformation. This book is an invitation to being alive together in reverence, to the sacred activism of beholding the divinity in all and embodying that awareness in ways that support the well-being of all creation. Every act of kindness, every offering of compassion, and every moment of conscious connection is a revolutionary act. Each step we take toward love and away from separation brings us closer to the new world that we've come to birth. When we walk the beauty way, we walk the new Earth into existence and become the ones who light the way.

The love in me bows to the love in you; may our shared love guide our collective way home.

CHAPTER 1: LOVE

"Close your eyes, fall in love, stay there."
~Rumi

I've never written a personal ad, but I've always thought that if I did, it would have just one line: "Must love dogs." Since I was little, I've felt a dimension of love in the depths of my being that the Persian poet Rumi calls "the bridge between you and everything." One of my earliest childhood memories is lying on the floor in my corduroy overalls with Winky, our beloved beagle mix. I was four years old, and I remember being so filled with devotion that I felt my love flowing from within like a vast and eternal wellspring, and I knew in that moment that this very feeling was the reason for, and greatest treasure of, being alive. I had a dawning awareness that he was mirroring something from deep within my innermost being that was precious, infinite, and transcended space and time. Receiving anything back from him was nowhere in my four-year-old consciousness, and my joy came from covering his sweet black nose in kisses as long as he would tolerate them while I whispered an ongoing wave of "I love you's" and gazed devotedly into his warm, brown eyes. Yet even then, I was aware that there was more, that the desire to communicate the infinitude of my love somehow was just the beginning, the opening of a sacred gateway.

Now, forty years later, in even deeper love with my sweet three-legged pup, Rumi, I find my heart ever more enchanted with this eternal fountain of rapture that bubbles up from within and is most often evoked by the canine soulmates and other more-than-human beings who have graced my life. This is a tribute to all the more-than-human beloveds who choose to be sacred mirrors of love along the earthly journey, opening our hearts and minds to a more integrous way of being alive. It's about a love that's too big to be contained within my own heart, the love we all share, the invisible thread of devotion that is the source of all nourishment, and the grace that connects us all. An extraordinary alchemy happens when we open our hearts to the wisdom of other kindred spirits in the natural realm. Truly, the greatest gift of being alive is the interconnection we share with all of existence, which Buddhist monk Thich Nhat Hahn described as our "interbeingness," as it is the key to the realization of our greatest potential both as individuals and as a collective field of consciousness.

This book draws inspiration from two of my most cherished companions, Rumi and Basil. These three-legged canine wonders have opened my heart to the vast ocean of grace available to us all through the love they have reflected back to me. It's fitting that the word "God" is "dog" spelled backward, as Rumi and Basil are such pure reflections of this divinity. This divinity loves us unconditionally and dwells eternally in every particle of creation. It is nourished in our own lives through the love we share with the ever-wise, ever-pure human and more-than-human wayshowers all around. Rumi and Basil opened my heart and soul in unimaginable ways, helping me remember the true essence of life. Whether you cherish cats, dogs, trees, or any other sacred beings in this living universe, my intention is that this tapestry of appreciation inspires your heart to open more fully to the blessings and grace on our shared journey of homecoming. This creation celebrates the divinity in all beings—canine, feline, equine, floral, solar, stellar, lunar, and beyond. It invites us to open our hearts to the wisdom and support from the more-than-human realm, guiding us in our collective transformation.

When I think of my love for Rumi, I sense it's more than love; it encompasses a feeling that any known human emotion can't adequately express. There's something about it that beckons from beyond the known. The magnitude of it breathes expansion into my edges. It begs me to let go of anything I've ever experienced before; it's here, in this invisible opening in the fabric of reality, that alchemy happens. Even a single moment of truly opening one's heart to be present with this frequency of love can set in motion a cascade of healing within and without as it begins to flow like nectar into the places of constriction that we may have tucked away long ago.

Chapter 1: Love

Love is our remedy, our answer, and our purpose.

It brings us back into wholeness, personally and collectively, which brings us into integrity. When we're living in integrity, in love, we're living on purpose. Humanity is evolving along with all of creation, and we can shape our future in profound ways by aligning our intentions and actions in the direction of harmony. Our past destructive habits and patterns are dissolving to make way for new, innovative, and creative ways to meet the needs of life on our dynamic planet. The wisdom and guidance offered by the more-than-human realm are profound; the intricate intelligence of natural living systems is astounding in its brilliant modeling of the power of cooperatively sharing resources as a pathway to peace.

We can be inspired to live more sustainably and harmoniously by studying how the natural world coexists in cooperative grace. We can learn from the way nutrients are shared in the complex root systems of forests, in the way trees make space for each other to share the sunlight, and in the way the mycelial network nourishes all of life through its millions of miles of interconnecting threads running just beneath the soil's surface. We can learn to make radical shifts in form and consciousness by marveling at the dragonfly's stunning transformation from a gray underwater nymph to a radiant, rainbow-colored, aerodynamic miracle. Similarly, we can observe how arid topsoil regenerates into nutrient-rich, life-giving loam through the art of composting.

We're being invited to make space in our hearts for the as yet unimagined, for the impossible made possible, as we open to a new paradigm in which wonder and awe guide us into a phenomenal new reality.

I see our beloved more-than-human companions as brilliant guides for us on this journey of awakening, as it's an evolution of our capacity to love, and they are gifted teachers in this realm of cooperative care. These dear ones are anchored in the reality of our interbeingness through a purity of heart and an awareness that hasn't been clouded with human technologies. In this book, I'll invite you to walk barefoot, kiss your favorite trees, talk with the stars, and sing from your soul with the birds, as enhancing our intimate connection with the wild world supports our sensorial embodied expansion. How our senses interpret the world around us guides us in our actions, and we can fuel our sensorial evolution through conscious communion with the natural realm to bring us into greater union with all of creation. There's a shift in embodiment happening, and as we soften our beliefs around what it means to be human, about why we're here, we let go of an expired concept of reality and open ourselves to something more beautiful than we've ever imagined.

This is an invitation into the grace of presence, the power of being fully alive together with the kindred spirits all around, seen and unseen, two-legged, three-legged, four-legged, and no-legged. It's an invitation to explore what it means to be human, how the senses can become a gateway into inter-dimensional wisdom, how starlight, tree leaves, coyote howls, warm breezes, raindrops, and all the other miraculous communications from the more-than-human realm are lighting the way to a new reality. They embody the language of cooperation and symbiosis, a language nearly lost in the over-consumption narrative that equates happiness with the next purchase or acquisition. Yet, this language endures, inviting us into the rich, sacred fertility of the present moment. This shimmering light of presence opens a doorway in the fabric of the Universe, a space for grace to enter, to illuminate the luscious garden of potential breathing in this holy now. In the early morning hum just before dawn, in the rising rhythm of woodpeckers in early spring, or in the caress of prayer flags on the breeze, there's but one song being sung.

We are part of an awakening intimacy, an alchemy of appreciation that bridges the dissolving old ways and a nascent new world of kindness and compassion called forth by the more-than-human kindred spirits around us.

We're all singing a universal song of love, and it's guiding us all home. I'm sharing this love letter from my heart to give back to the more-than-human realm, the Earth and cosmos, the love that is the source of all existence, even a fraction of the grace I've received. And that I still receive; as I write, I'm gazing out on a sea of green in the budding trees surrounding our woodland sanctuary, marveling at the symphony of birdsong and quietude, the exquisite majesty of forest, sky, and light interweaving in a dance of life-giving beauty. I pause, look up, and smile, realizing that I'm evolving in this very moment, feeling my heart open as I offer gratitude and awe for the quiet blessings continuously being offered by the seen and unseen energies of creation. I feel a softening in my mind and in my breath as I wonder what else is possible. I am open to becoming as attuned to those around me as these trees are to the sacred ecosystem of which they are a part. Can we begin to live with the intention of building harmony and shifting our patterns to create habits of kindness that build systems of compassion and guide us into a world of care? Yes, we can; we're being guided, and it's what we're here for.

Writing this book was a training in this very practice, as every day I needed to pause, look up to the treetops, listen to the birds, savor the breeze on my skin, call on my ancestors and angels, give thanks, surrender, and open to something new and magnificent. As I write now, looking out into the national forest on a gorgeous summer day, the breeze blowing through the canopy while the subtle green light sparkles down all around us, I'm aware of how our sight, and therefore our perspective, is transforming. The rods and cones in our eyes are evolving to be able to process and integrate the new codes in the photonic light coming from the increase in solar flares, CMEs (coronal mass ejections), and all the other incoming cosmic light. This process is divinizing our sight; as we allow the inner eye to focus on the truth of our oneness, we transform the world. It's already transforming as more and more souls awaken to the reality of our interconnectedness and to the profound beauty and power this holds for us as a planetary whole and integral part of a universal ecosystem of living consciousness.

We are being divinized by the light; ascension is a transformative process, alchemizing our narrative of separation into an appreciation of our unity and our cooperative capacity to thrive.

Allow any grief to process as the old world falls away, and invite in your creativity and hope for the new one that's emerging. I've known deep grief, and I've come to the awareness that grief and creativity go hand in hand—the letting go and honoring of what was carving sacred and fertile space for what is next. As we see old paradigms dissolving around us and the chaos and pain that can accompany such radical transformation, we're invited to open our souls to what's possible, what could come to be, what may never have even been imagined before. Now is the time to open our hearts to each other, to open our minds to the wisdom of the natural world, and to open our collective consciousness to the brilliance of the cosmos.

The natural world is showing us how to live from the heart, in the subtle realm where the divine dwells, in the wisdom our ancestors knew. It's only been in the past few thousand years that we've shifted away from this knowing as we've been navigating the Kali Yuga, the time of forgetting. Now, we're entering into the Age of Aquarius, a time of awakening to and remembering who we truly are as creator beings of love. *Kiakahi* is a Hawaiian term that describes one's sacred purpose; I sense our collective kiakahi is to fully embrace our sacredness and that of all life in the Universe, as a way of coming into wholeness through devoted cooperation.

I could define my life chapters by the devotion I've felt with the canine beloveds who have walked beside me. I'm aware of how, with each relationship, the love I've shared with them has shaped and evolved me into a wiser, more compassionate version of myself. This soul-to-soul communion, this sacred mirroring that our interbeingness draws forth, is a channel for the divine to infuse us with the grace that's sculpting us into the new humanity we're here to become.

These holy midwives appear as our beloved companions—whether they walk on three or four legs, as felines, canines, equines, or as our gentle plant and aquatic allies. They manifest as the cosmos guiding the rhythms of our world, as the sacred roses and dandelions adorning our days with beauty, and as the bluebirds serenading us into the birth of a new day. All these cherished beings, nurturing us with care, kinship, and sustenance, are leading us toward the realization of a new paradigm that harmonizes with all of creation. This gorgeous planet has more than enough resources to abundantly care for those dwelling here, and we're being invited to live more mindfully and heartfully so that all may be well-fed and well-loved. Perhaps you can relate to this with your canine, feline, or any other sacred companion: The more-than-human connections that bless our lives are often the most heart-opening and wisdom-inspiring. This book is a love story of gratitude for the miracle of these relationships and the gifts of awakening they offer to us. It's an invitation to evolve collectively, consciously aligning ourselves with all of existence, recognizing the same kinship we share with our beloved, more-than-human companions in every aspect of life around us.

There is a love language beyond the confines of human linguistics that causes a surge of life-force energy to flood through our bodies and ignite the passion of presence in our souls.

It's the one that's spoken in the turquoise sparkling of a cresting wave, in the soft caress of a summer breeze wafting through the pine trees, and in the intoxicating scent of the first honeysuckle blossoming on the mountaintop. It's in the touch of moonlight on our bare skin and the peace we feel leaning back into the welcoming arms of our favorite tree. It's in the precious communion we feel with our beloved canine, feline, and equine companions, the depth of pure love and presence we know when we gaze into their eyes and feel our hearts in union. The blessing of these intimacies opens us to remember that we share this sacred connection with all of creation. We're in a time of incredible awakening on our planet. We're witnessing the old world of separation dissolving and shifting into the emergence of a new era wherein honoring the sacredness of our interconnection is guiding us forward. When we look back in time, we see that those who have survived and thrived in times of great transformation, such as this one, are the ones who have focused on living cooperatively and in right relationship.

As Elisabet Sahtouris shared in an interview with Astrologer Heather Ensworth, the Darwinian theory of evolution only illustrates a youthful phase marked by competition. As Sahtouris explains, when we look back over the last four billion years of the Earth's evolution, we see that ecosystems of competition evolved into ecosystems of cooperation, such as single cells evolving into nucleated cells, which then became multicellular creatures like dinosaurs, dolphins, and humans. When competition matured into cooperation, evolutionary leaps occurred, and systems evolved from the survival mode to the thriving mode. As we observe the crumbling of a patriarchal culture, we're being guided by the divine intelligence of the natural realm in the birthing of a new and more harmonious way of coexisting on the incredible blue-green jewel of a planet we call home. We're being invited to decenter ourselves and release the supremacist consciousness that humans are the center of existence, which has allowed for the exploitation of the myriad other lifeforms with whom we share this world and has brought us collectively to the brink of destruction. This creates space for us to step into a new consciousness of care and collaboration to birth a more just and harmonious existence for all.

I'm devoted to exploring how we can allow our interbeingness to inspire all of our relatedness, to expand our family circle to include all of creation. Mother Teresa said, "The problem with the world is that we draw the circle of our family too small." When we surrender to this awareness and allow ourselves to be transformed by it, we can release the limited binary thinking that has led to so much division and destruction. The evolution to embracing all of creation as our family is the gateway to birthing a new way of being, one in which compassion and consideration for all life light our way forward. Consciousness and form inform one another; everything in the natural world constantly communicates and adapts based on what's happening in the ecosystem. This is the glorious phenomenon of symbiosis, the law of interconnection that weaves all of life into a web of co-creation in every breath, raindrop, and thought. If it feels good, I'd love to invite you to pause and look up to the sky, savoring a deep breath and offering a wave of gratitude for the countless blessings being bestowed upon you in this very moment through the grace of sunlight, gravity, photosynthesis, and all of the other miraculous occurrences happening to support your existence. Pausing, giving thanks, and inviting connection to the vast living consciousness that is the very source of our aliveness opens the doorway to being fully open and available for the grace of this majestic, collaborative awakening.

This living consciousness gently invites us to remember and embody this ineffable grace even more fully, gently alchemizing our sense of separation into an awareness of the unconditional love that unites us all. It's the eternal fountain of divinity beneath the stories of division we may have been taught that is ever-present and infinite. This is an invitation to relax any limited concepts of self and life and open to expanding possibilities for fulfilling our shared dharma to birth a new paradigm of harmony.

It's a collective messiah this time; it's the collaborative voice of the natural world and all of us who are awakening and making the conscious choice to live more gently on the planet.

From an astrological standpoint, the Piscean Age of separation and domination is ending as we begin a new processional cycle, the Age of Aquarius. The Age of Aquarius is centered in harmony and guided by respect for all of creation and will carry us forward into the next twenty-four thousand years of our existence. From a geological perspective, the time we're stepping into is known as the Symbiocene Era, in which harmony is the focus and is realized through cooperative evolution and interdependent collaboration.

Both the Earth and the cosmos are inviting us into radical transformation, into a revolution of love marked by the birthing of a new paradigm of care for all of creation.

We're in our infancy as an evolving version of humanity, and much more is possible. As we shift from a state of contraction to a state of softening into the safety of belonging that is at the heart of our inter-beingness, we can open to new ways of coexisting that are mutually life-enhancing. It's a coming together of hearts and souls, both human and more-than-human, that creates such a powerful wave of love that it shifts the trajectory for all life on Earth. The new light coming in from the Sun and the cosmos supports the awakening of our multidimensional awareness and activates our crystalline light bodies. This means that our carbon-based forms are changing, as our density is lightening, and we are shifting from being Homo Sapiens to being Homo Luminous beings of light. What does this actually mean? As the Sun becomes more active and radiates new photonics into our magnetosphere, the energy field around the Earth informs how we experience life, and our bodies integrate this new energy. As a result, our three-dimensional forms evolve to hold the new light, and reality is transformed. We're witnessing changes in what we're drawn to consume and how we're called to live as we're inspired to explore new avenues of embodiment. There's a rebalancing happening as we remember the wisdom of our matriarchal ancestors, whose focus was on cooperation and celebrating the divine feminine and divine masculine in harmony while honoring the union of the Earth and cosmos in supreme reverence.

We get to choose which path we take as a collective, and it hinges on where we direct our attention. We're in a time of remembering why we're here, moving beyond the limitations of dualistic perceptions to come into greater wholeness. It's not a transcendent journey; it's an earthly, embodied journey of embracing the beauty of our interconnectedness and the call to action inspired by that awareness. The Greek term *kosmos* speaks to the beauty inherent in the way the celestial energies move in harmony; when we tune the instrument of our aliveness to the kosmos, the harmony of the spheres, we become that beauty, that expression of love humming in resonance with all that is. The journey leads nowhere but here; we're at a crossroads, and we can choose the beauty way, an embodiment of the sacred that mirrors the holiness in all. This divine embodiment comes alive when we feel safe enough to be soft and real, and in that softening, something magnificent happens. The layers of protection and constriction we've been holding within us begin to transform, and a new aliveness emerges. The safety we feel with our more-than-human companions, with our sweet kittens and pups, with the wildflowers and butterflies, with the warmth of the rising Sun, allows us to remember this ability to soften, to evolve through love, and to more fully embody our true nature as divine light in human form, reflecting that to all with whom we constellate.

We're being invited to interrupt our collective patterns of perception and rearrange our belief systems of who we think we are to open ourselves to something so much more expansive.

We're in a death/rebirth cycle; our transformation is a return to our innate goodness as perfect, whole, and complete, where we recognize the divinity in all those with whom we share this journey. What's the best that can happen? We can choose to wake up and start living in greater integrity with our soul's purpose, which is to create a more just world. We can let go of the limited thinking that has kept us from feeling the grace of this sense of belonging, and we can open ourselves to becoming so much more than we thought we were. May this very breath carry you into deeper intimacy with the true self pulsing in every cell of your being, this sacred love that is your true nature and unites us all in a rainbow web of boundless potentiality.

Rupert Sheldrake, an English biologist, suggests that much of our earthly experience is the result of morphogenetic fields, the fields of consciousness that guide our existence through a sense of habits and memories that get passed down from generation to generation in like systems, such as trees, humans, flowers, or any other similar group of beings, causing patterns of behavior and ways of being. Sheldrake's research supports the idea that we can influence these habits of behavior and, therefore, shift what we might have considered "laws" of nature through conscious collaboration that leads to radical evolutionary shifts. When we look at the neural network among plants and the mycelial web among fungi, we see the vast and brilliant interconnection of all life on Earth. There's a living consciousness in our shared field; it took us over 13 billion years of evolution to get to this moment, and we can influence the direction of our current evolutionary trajectory by choosing to live in a way that honors the intimate interconnection of all of existence. This wisdom is in the essence of all life on the planet, and it's through opening the heart that we realize the beauty and power in this awareness as a guiding light to a new way of being. As we allow our hearts to be opened by the brilliant, more-than-human souls all around us who are already attuned to this truth, our human morphogenetic field will transform, and we as a species can evolve to become a source of creative harmony in the world.

Animism is the awareness that everything is alive, and this understanding offers a wise compass as we navigate our personal and collective metamorphosis. It directs us on how to live well on Earth with our family, which encompasses all of creation. It addresses the vital energy animating all things, encouraging a perspective broad enough to acknowledge this vitality in both the visible and invisible realms, in ancestral dimensions, and in the fertile expanses of life that may remain unnamed but can be sensed with open-hearted awareness. *Puhpowee*, the Anishinaabe term for "the force that causes mushrooms to push up from the earth overnight," speaks to the mysterious grace that is the source of the animistic miracle in which we currently dwell.

In the living world, there is an ongoing exchange of wild wisdom among biofields, and magic happens in these sacred communions.

In this time of deep regeneration, we're being invited to a quantum leap in consciousness by choosing to live in right relationship with the natural world and allowing this reverence to guide us into new ways of living in harmony with all of creation. Our more-than-human relatives are sacred way-showers on this journey of awakening, and it's through the love they offer that we're being inspired to remember who we really are.

This is a romance of life, a tale of grace, *asha* (Sanskrit for hope), and *manaʻoʻio* (Hawaiian for faith). The translation of manaʻoʻio is "to take your mana (internal and infinite power within) and throw it as high as the io (hawk) can soar." What a gorgeous invitation; just writing about it inspired me to pause, take a deep breath, and, with all my heart, launch my mana in full faith up into the infinite expanse of sky above. Some of my most profound learnings have come from indigenous wisdom traditions, and I have deep respect and gratitude for my teachers and the blessings I've received from these sacred schools of awareness. Hawaiian and Sanskrit are deeply woven into my consciousness; they bring extraordinary richness to the lexicon of my reality in how they expand concepts to include more multidimensional understandings of our lived experiences. It's my hope that their presence in this offering will awaken new neural pathways to connect us all more intimately in a shared language of light in addition to honoring the wisdom of these ancient lineages. Thus, you will occasionally meet them throughout this text, as they're an integral part of my internal dialogue. I find that they often illustrate my lived experience more wholeheartedly than the English language alone can. *Mahalo* (Hawaiian for thank you) for being on this journey with me, and *aloha kea kua* (the unfathomable divinity of me recognizes the unfathomable divinity of you).

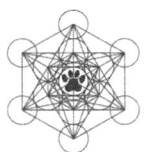

Soul Nourishment

The Hawaiian word for faith, *mana' o'i o,* invites us to surrender our greatest desires up to the heavens, to the unseen forces collaborating to bring our dreams into reality through the art of trusting enough to hand it all over. What do you desire so deeply that you're willing to hand it over, to practice the art of faith through loosening your grip and inviting in support? What action(s) can you explore that reflect this great letting go? When you do so, how do you feel in your body and in your mind? Take some space to journal about the somatic sensations and awareness that arise as a result of turning something so precious over to the unfathomable divinity that is all around.

Kiakahi is the Hawaiian word that describes our sacred purpose. What emerges when you breathe the vibration of kiakahi deep into your bones, remembering the brilliance of your essence and listening to the song of your soul? Take some space to journal about how your kiakahi might be ready to evolve, perhaps to new heights or even into something you've never imagined before, allowing yourself to have faith in your creative inspirations and receive support from the incredible benevolence that is the living Universe. When you're finished, offer a silent thank you for the help and grace that's already on the way.

CHAPTER 2: SOULMATES

"Wherever you are and whatever you do, be in love."
~Rumi

It was Valentine's Day, and I was journaling in front of the fireplace. My heart was still aching from what had felt like a challenging period of life with the death of my beloved pup, Basil, the unexpectedly painful ending of a relationship, and the depth of grief that accompanied both. Pen in hand, my attention was suddenly drawn to the watercolor portrait of Basil that graced the bed where he'd spent his last months; I heard him silently say, "Now."

I'd asked him during his final earthly days to let me know when it would be time to welcome another canine love into my life, and several months later, it was time. At that moment, I picked up my phone, and a message from my father came through. He'd sent me a fundraising letter from our local Humane Society with a Valentine's Day theme featuring an enchanting photo accompanying the story of "Valentine," an eight-month-old mini-Labrador mix who'd been rescued from severe trauma and was seeking her forever home. Her story was almost identical to Basil's—early-stage severe neglect and trauma that resulted in her being taken in by the Humane Society and needing intense care, including a leg amputation in order to save her life. Her bright eyes and radiant smile in the photo beamed love straight into my soul, and instantly, I knew she was the one, my heart opening like a wild rose to the miracle that would change my life forever.

The next day, I found myself in the front office of our local Humane Society, my heart brimming with the anticipation of meeting the one I knew was about to be my new soulmate. My mother had come with me, and we both melted in delight when Rumi came hopping and wiggling down the hall, her smiling eyes greeting us as if she'd always known we were coming for her. It was an instant yes all around, her soft snuggles and gentle kisses affirming her approval, my full body smile revealing that I was completely smitten. Six days later, released from her surgical convalescence, she rode home with me to begin what has been one of the richest and most magical adventures of my life.

I had spent the days leading up to her arrival deep-cleaning the house as if I was preparing for a saint, blessing every corner and fine-tuning the energy in a way I never had before. I was laughing internally as I washed the windows for the first time in ages, yet I understood on a deeper level the power of the clear, sacred space that was needed for the dimension of healing that would be required for her. When I arrived back at the shelter, her doctor handed me a thick folder detailing the long list of medications she was on and told me that because she was also being treated for heartworm (the youngest case they'd ever seen), she would need to be kept calm and on a leash for the next three months. I reeled a little at the thought that this sweet puppy, who had been unable to run and play for many weeks, would be restricted for another three months, and I felt an even deeper commitment to supporting her complete recovery and creating an amazing new life for her.

When we arrived at the house that afternoon, she knew instantly that she was home, walking around purposefully, sniffing and assessing the space with an air of approval and deep satisfaction. When bedtime came later that evening, she went and stood with determined intention next to my bed, giving no attention whatsoever to the plush dog bed I'd arranged for her on the floor. She looked me in the eye with clarity and a hint of reprimand as I laughingly gathered her in my arms and settled her in lovingly so she could rest her little head on my pillow.

When I climbed in soon after, my heart was overflowing at feeling her complete sense of peace; she was curled up blissfully as if she had spent every night of her life there. Hours later, I woke to find us entwined, her skinny little legs stick-straight around my neck, and my arms stretched out around her shaved, stitches-covered body. My heart melted in love, my whole being reveling in the frequency of home that I felt resonating deep in her bones and radiating out in her soft, contented exhalations of gratitude as she snoozed peacefully through the night.

Her entrance into my world shifted everything. There's a dimension of grace that comes from parenting a more-than-human being that brings such a depth of fulfillment, which is possibly even greater for those who aren't parenting human children. It was my first adoption as a single parent, as the other dogs in my life had come to me while I was living in partnership, and the instant bonding that happened between Rumi and me was beyond anything I'd ever experienced. On that first night home, as she fell asleep with her head on my pillow and a beatific smile on her face, my heart melted even more in the sweet grace of knowing I'd been chosen to be her forever mama. We woke up the next morning to cuddles and kisses, singing two songs that instantly became part of the daily wake-up routine that's become one of the sweetest parts of our day. From day one, we've shared sweet rituals that have deepened our soul connection and have been an integral part of her healing journey. Starting and ending the day devotionally with her has cultivated a spiritual foundation in our relationship that's developed into something so vastly nourishing and expansive for both of us, and it's opened the door to a dimension of connection that only deepens with each day. Our cuddles and affirmations in the morning are just as sweet as the bedtime routine where she puts on her PJs (takes off her collar), plays a rousing game of hide-and-seek that involves practicing her sniffing skills by sleuthing out the treats I've hidden around the bedroom, and then has her teeth brushed and gets tucked in with kisses and blessings until she sleepily grumbles at me to let her rest. Gratitude and prayers are shared before we both drift off to sleep, appreciative and held in the arms of love.

Morning often begins when she gently wakes me, ready for breakfast, offering quiet meows until I reach over, rub her velvety ears, and slowly rise. She has the sweetest voice, and rarely does she bark, though she has a dazzling range of communication styles, many of which have a catlike quality and land more in the meow range. She also has a surprisingly rich array of tones and notes. I've never heard another dog with her capability for vocal variance and communication, and her vocalizations often bring me to devoted laughter, especially the sleepy ones that open my heart in more ways than I can count. She knows how much I love them, and I think she intentionally generates them to fuel my adoration. I usually ask her to sit before receiving meals or treats, and her "come on, mom"-esque grumbles for me to hurry it up always leave me smiling. Just as enchanting to me is the way she curls herself up in a tiny donut shape, her nose tucked into her tail, the circle of her form littler than most thirty-pound pups because she folds her body in where her leg is missing to create an even smaller ball of fur and sweetness. Because she's had her back right leg amputated, she isn't able to scratch her right side at all, so I make a point to thoroughly scratch that side from head to toe a few times a day, and the relief and gratitude that shine in her eyes is nectar for my soul. She's heightened my awareness of the gift of being able to pay attention to what someone might need to feel more comfortable, anticipating it before they even ask, and the mutual appreciation that comes with the beauty of creating greater wellness for another. This feels especially sacred with our beloveds who don't communicate in human language, and to attune ourselves to hearing these unspoken desires and needs is an art that can profoundly change the way we're able to live together as a collective. To anticipate the needs of a pup, a baby, an elder, or a tree and to offer support, care, and love creates a ripple effect that enhances all of life on Earth.

However, I don't have to anticipate Rumi's needs too often, as she's excellent at communicating her desires and doesn't shy away from expressing them. She's the first canine companion I've had who seems to have an agenda and plan for most of her days, and she doesn't have much tolerance when I'm not on the same page. Thus, when she says it's playtime—which is often—as much as I can, I try to pause whatever I'm doing and meet her in that space. I realized early on that she was a being who would need lots of stimulation, attention, activity, and fun—more than any other dog I'd had before. In truth, all of our beloved companions deserve this level of care, and Rumi's hope is that through sharing some of our stories, others will be inspired to elevate the love and attention they offer to the dear ones they care for.

Rumi is extremely intelligent, and the more I've supported and encouraged this quality in her, the more it's developed. She absolutely adores her toys, treasuring each one. She holds them between her paws, admiring them with delight, and rolls on her back with a big smile, happily chattering to herself to enhance the enjoyment. While the therapeutic benefits of being present in love with our more-than-human beloveds create waves of beneficial energies for our nervous systems—from the activation of oxytocin when cuddling to the dopamine that begins to flow when playing—simply being present with her and witnessing her evolution has been one of the greatest gifts of her entrance into my world. Even putting a meal down before her or offering one of the many treats she gets throughout the day brings joy to my heart, and I can feel the mutual exchange of appreciation between us palpably contributing to something so much larger than just us. Any love we share with another is feeding the larger wave of grace that's shaping our collective reality, yet I sense that these exchanges with our more-than-human relatives are nurturing something extra special in the web of light connecting us all.

A new world is birthing, one wherein we all feel safe together, and I sense that the love we share with our more-than-human companions is fine-tuning our frequency, calibrating us to a new level of loving awareness that's key to the evolutionary leap in consciousness we're being invited to embrace as a collective.

Winky, the first pup love in my life, was a beautiful introduction to this vibration of loving awareness inherent in the human and more-than-human connection. He was alive in the days when it was more typical for dogs to roam freely, and he had a morning routine of trotting to a neighbor's house about a block away, where he would receive country ham for breakfast. Every morning, he would sweetly connect with me before heading out, and upon his return, we would share a mutual delight that was unlike anything I'd experienced with the humans in my life, gazing deeply into each other's eyes while I covered him in kisses and wrapped my arms around his welcoming, warm body. His days were mostly spent exploring outside with me and kindly allowing me to dress him up in various wigs and hats and sunglasses, or resting peacefully while I stared deeply into his eyes, kissing his perfect silky ears and feeling a love that felt infinite and inexhaustible. I remember feeling like I couldn't ever kiss him enough, of being so smitten with his nose, his paws, his softness that it couldn't ever possibly be fully expressed. What inspires that depth of devotion, of presence and unconditional love if not the very essence of grace radiating between the two hearts connecting in that sacred space? It's been my experience that our more-than-human kindred naturally invite this frequency of pure loving connection, and they mirror its aliveness within our own hearts when we're present enough to feel it. The natural world longs for this intimacy with us, this true connection, that opens doors to levels of co-creation from the heart. It is in this connection that we have the ability to birth new dimensions of consciousness, ones that can expand us beyond our limited ways of perceiving the world and guide us into more cooperative, harmonious ways of being alive together. There's something about sensorial connection, the sharing of touch through savoring the soft fur of a beloved cat or dog, or inhaling the rich and delicate scent of a rose, or being serenaded by the delicious breeze before an evening rainstorm. These sensory connections and spaces of conscious appreciation and reception serve as gateways to expanding our subtle awareness. They tap into the extrasensory field of knowing, allowing us to transcend established ways of being and open ourselves to new experiences that deepen our alignment with the sacredness of our own existence and all of life.

Attachment theory is a therapeutic concept that helps us understand relational patterns, and it's often limited to relationships between humans and other humans. When we expand it to include our more-than-human kindred, we recognize the beauty and richness of the more-than-human beings who have helped us on our path by offering the stability and security that we couldn't find in our human relationships growing up. Sometimes these more-than-human soulmates show up for us in ways that humans aren't even capable of, as was the case with my beloved Spike, a sweet, shaggy black terrier mix who followed me home one early summer day when I was ten. Our bond was instant, and his devotion to me was indescribable; it was as if we had been together for lifetimes. After only a brief meeting as I was riding my bicycle past his original home, he committed himself to me, escaping from his backyard every day to trek over a mile to get to me. After weeks of taking him back home to his original family every day, they said that he clearly preferred me over them and offered for my family to adopt him, to which we instantly agreed. He became my constant companion and best friend, and when, many years later, I returned home after a month in the hospital following a near-death experience, he never left my bedside. He sat with me day and night, the best nursemaid one could ever hope for, and to this day, I know that much of my miraculous healing was due to his devotion and loving care. I remember the feeling of his soft, silky black fur in my fingers when I first returned home. I felt a wave of heart opening and homecoming in my system that brought me back into my body for the first time in the many weeks since my car wreck. Looking into his eyes that evening as he lay cuddling in bed with me, our hearts breathing in grateful unison, I felt a part of my soul return home that had felt lost in the trauma and impossible to locate up until that moment with him back in my arms. These dear ones are such angels, harbingers of the heart awakening that we're here for collectively as a planet, soulmates who help us remember who we are and why we're here. They're wise teachers who steadfastly mirror our divinity to us even as we forget, over and over, unwavering in their love and resolute in their devotion.

What if we allowed ourselves to be so touched by this beauty and truth of existence that we all lived from this space, committed as soulmates to all of creation, making choices that honored this sacred union? Our world would be a reflection of cooperation and kindness, which is the new world that's birthing, the Symbiocene Era dawning before us and from within us, emerging through every heartful communion and moment of loving presence that we share with all of the life surrounding us.

Sweet Spike passed into the *parinirvana*, the luminous field of the beyond, at the amazing age of eighteen, breathing his last breath in my arms as we lay together in a beam of golden morning light. I held him for what seemed like hours after he had shared his final breath, nurturing the sacred expansion of his precious and radiant soul, and in that rich and holy space, I finally understood the reality that we are not contained by these bodies. It was clear that our essence exists long after we've dropped our forms, and that the love and connection we share with those who have gone beyond can be just as strong, sometimes even stronger, even if the breath has stopped and the body has been released. Thank you, Spike, my love. As I share this, I sense you here with me in a way I haven't in decades. I feel your loving presence in the trees swaying in the wind, in the soft caress of the breeze against my bare legs and the tears rolling down my cheeks as I write. Thank you. Thank you for the way you showed me how I could be loved, for showing me what devotion looks like, for awakening me to the beauty of how love continues eternally, unbound by earthly limitations, and is an ongoing source of evolutionary nourishment for the spirit. As I'm writing, a hummingbird is flying up, coming in close and chirping while gazing deep into my eyes, then flying to the nearby oak, then back to me, over and over. I hear a high-pitched *cheep* and look down to see a tiny sparrow resting right at my feet, her soft tuft of honey-colored bird fur accentuating the clear, focused connection that her shiny, black eyes are commanding from me. The tears roll freely as I bow, ever-awed at the magnificence of the way the natural world responds, at how simply remembering the depth of my love with Spike has invoked his presence so profoundly that I'm energetically brought to my knees, while my more-than-human kindred show up all around me to confirm the magic, to say, *yes, open your heart, and we'll bless you even more fully with our presence and love.* Dear winged ones, thank you. Spike, are you that hummingbird? Winky, are you that sweet sparrow? As D. R. Butler said, "The world is as we see it. There is no limit to what is available right now. Right now, we can open up to everything."

Soon after Spike's transition, my heart opening continued when Henry and Basil, the first two dogs I parented as a young adult, came into my life. They blessed me in the ways they awakened me to caregiving, and they taught me so much about what it truly means to love unconditionally. I was twenty-three when Henry came into my world; she was a high-spirited, sassy strawberry blonde who I instantly fell for when we met at the Humane Society. We journeyed together for the next fourteen years, during which she was a divine mirror to my humanness and taught me volumes about parenting and communicating from the heart. Several friends mentioned throughout our journey together that Henry had clearly chosen me, as not everyone would have been able to stay by her side due to her unusual personality and bouts of aggression. I'm in awe of the ways she helped me grow as a person in my capacity to hold space for her healing and nurture her into a life of peace. Henry, you were one of my greatest teachers, and I'm more grateful for our journey together than words can ever express.

A year after Henry came into my world, Basil arrived. I was teaching at the local university, and a student in one of my classes shared that they had just rescued a dog at the Humane Society where she worked who had had to have one of his front legs amputated to save his life. Upon hearing his story, I instantly knew he and I were destined to be together. The next day, my girlfriend and I drove out to meet him, and an hour later, he was in the car with us, heading to his new forever home. Everyone loved Basil. He was an adorable russet-colored little Sheba Enu mix whose sweetness charmed everyone he met. He embodied the divine masculine in the most beautiful ways, his softness and steadfastness radiated a sense of safety, and his gently protective nature was deeply soothing for everyone he encountered. He was small but mighty. He was missing his front left leg, so his hindquarters were extremely muscular, and because his lifestyle with me was so active, his form was that of a little bodybuilder.

When he first came home from the shelter, he was still in the midst of integrating the many months of trauma he had just been through, and it was exquisite to witness the slow and gentle opening of his heart as he realized how safe and deeply loved he was in his new home. Within weeks, he had blossomed into the most loving, adoring little pup, regaining his physical strength and mobility as his spirit shone forth with a magnitude of gratitude that was uplifting to everyone he met. After Henry's transition from the Earth plane, Basil and I journeyed together for two more years, and that final year with him was one of the most powerful years of my life. I was already in the space of deep personal transformation, feeling like I was walking between worlds as I shed outworn patterns and perceptions while navigating the liminality of not yet having landed on new footing. His steady, loving presence is, to this day, one of the greatest gifts I've ever known. I can still feel his thick, soft red fur and see his calm, grounding gaze as he stared deep into my soul, knowing me more fully than perhaps I even knew myself. To be held and known that way is a rare treasure, and it changed me forever. The last few months of his life were a holy portal of devotion, with me holding his paw and supporting his soul with all my heart as he prepared to return to the arms of his beloved. His bones are now buried right outside the door of our forest sanctuary, and every day I'm blessed to breathe beside him and feel his eternally loving presence guiding our way with devoted care.

It often seems that these intimate companionships are orchestrated by a higher wisdom that blesses us with delightful and often unexpected connections at exactly the right moment. Just as Spike chose me so many years ago, Peaches is the charming cat who walked into my mother's backyard one day like an angel straight from heaven. At the time, my eighty-three-year-old mother was beginning her journey of cognitive and physical evolution known as dementia, and she was navigating significant physical and psycho-emotional challenges. My sisters and I were doing everything we could to support her wellness, but we couldn't seem to resolve the fear and loneliness that had suddenly infiltrated her world. We'd suggested a cat companion, though my mother was adamantly opposed every time it was mentioned, declaring that she "wasn't a cat person" and instead musing about having a dog, which for many reasons wouldn't have been possible at that time. Serendipitously, a sweet orange tabby cat began crossing through her backyard every afternoon, quietly passing along the edge of the garden almost as if he didn't want to be noticed. When we reached out, he would shyly disappear into the bushes, though would return again the next day, again passing silently by and sidestepping any connection. Then one day, he was offered a bite of her lunch, and everything changed. He began coming daily and offering himself up for petting, sometimes purring and rubbing against her legs, and our hearts instantly opened to his sweet, gentle nature. Within weeks, he was living with her, happily ensconced on a pile of pillows on her bed and enjoying the luxury of her utter devotion and care. My entire family has fallen in love with him, and his presence has completely changed my mother's world in all of the best ways. Having another soul to care for and share life with has opened and enlivened her in ways I couldn't have imagined, and the bond they share has supercharged her spirit and nourished her soul beyond anything I could have hoped for. Her energy came back, her joy reemerged, and some of her strength returned. While many other cats have blessed my life, it's Peaches who has touched me the most deeply with his precious feline magic and opened me even more fully to the sacred wisdom and love of our leonine beloveds.

Whether it's a cat, a dog, a horse, or any other beloved life companion, these holy ones are such beautiful teachers for helping us remember how to love fully, inclusively, and beyond any unhelpful sense of separation based on categories of embodiment. There's a thread of commonality among the more-than-human dear ones with whom we journey, as they all seem to nourish within us a capacity for caring that's one of the most important accomplishments we can hope to achieve in this lifetime. The evolutionary development that's come from being able to nurture and encourage Rumi on her journey has been one of the biggest blessings on my path. The depth of parenting that she invites has far surpassed any other parenting I've done with previous pups, and the joy that's inspired in my heart has been one of the most rewarding experiences of my life. From day one, she's required a level of attention and care that's nonnegotiable; she's clear in who she is and what she wants, and the strength of her character commands full presence in every moment. Because she required so much more care than any other dog companion I'd had because of where she was in her healing, the bond we formed was deeper than what I'd experienced previously. And because of where I was in my own healing, it was beautifully restorative to have someone with whom to share my love and devotion, and we found ourselves in a rich space of adoration that has only deepened as the years go by. Soulmates come in many forms, and I see clearly how loving her has healed me. How you see anything is how you see everything, and from day one, I knew that she and I had been brought together in the sweetest destiny by unseen forces of grace.

This was echoed a few months after she'd come into my life when we were on one of our daily visits to the preschool down the road. Rumi adores all children; she melts for them, and they for her. To meet her desire to be with little people before we moved out to the woods, each morning, I would walk her to the preschool down the street from our home. The toddlers would see us coming and run to the playground's edge, their arms stretched out and their faces beaming at us, smiling at Rumi's open heart and wagging tail coming to meet them. As we neared,

Rumi's gait would evolve into a full-body wag, her body swinging to-and-fro with a wide grin stretched across her face and her ears pressed back against her head in delight. One day, one of the teachers asked how we'd met. As I shared the tale of our Valentine's Day reunion, she reflected, with a sparkle in her eye, "You two are a match made in heaven." Smiling in agreement, I gave a silent thank you to Basil and all of the other invisible forces of love who had indeed brought us together. I believe that all of the ones with whom we share the life journey are divinely assigned for our soul's growth and evolution, and acknowledging this opens a channel for even more intentional collaboration with the energies helping to orchestrate these sacred connections. I sense this hand of grace in all of our relationships, human and more-than-human, though I've often felt it most powerfully in the canine and feline companions who have blessed my life.

This is our book, a collaboration between me and Rumi and the other more-than-human beloveds who have shaped my life and continue to evolve me in the most extraordinary ways. Often when I sit down to write, Rumi snuggles into me in ways she rarely ever does, lying under the table where I write, her head resting on my feet like a pillow, or tucked in as close as she can possibly be, her head resting on my knee and gazing up at me endearingly, knowing I'm going to lean down and kiss her on the nose as often as I can. Sometimes, I ask her what she has to say, and when I did just now, her reply was, "There is so much available to all of us right now if we choose to be present for it. We can open our awareness to smiling more, enjoying more love with all of our companions, playing, snuggling, savoring, and really listening." This is true wisdom. She invites me daily to put down my plan and shift my focus to playtime, to songs and dancing together, to going out to savor the trees and the scents in the air together, to offer and receive more affection, and to ask what would bring her greater joy and well-being. One of my favorite things to do is to go up to her while she's sleeping and silently leave a treat under her nose. No need to earn or deserve love; they're on tap here. We can offer that to all beings, celebrating them for no reason other than simply because they exist. We can practice that with ourselves, too. Right now, you could pause and give yourself a hug, congratulate yourself simply for existing in this moment exactly as you are, and then gift yourself with a smile, feeling the endorphins that naturally start to flow from the simple act of smiling, infusing your cells with feel-good hormones and elevating your well-being. Love is right here, right now; all we need to do is open ourselves to it, and give thanks. The natural realm is modeling this for us all the time, surrounding us with clean air to breathe and applauding us with the rustling of tree leaves in the breeze, the enchanting beauty of blossoming flowers, and rivers flowing with clean, healing waters. As I pause and gaze out into the forest, the trees are breathing inspiration into me as a gentle breeze sings through the canopy and gently caresses my bare skin, the plants and air and Sun softening my heart and infusing me with gratitude for lifetimes.

I've been a narrator my whole life; I remember being seven years old, playing in the woods behind my childhood home, immersed in ongoing silent storytelling of what my character was doing. I often cast myself with a different name and gender, though it was me, doing exactly what I was doing, making walnut peace pipes, building treehouses and tipis, creating fairy ecosystems with twigs and grass, all the while being in deep and intimate collaboration with the natural world around me. I had a lot of freedom growing up; both of my parents worked, and I had two older sisters, so I was granted the freedoms they had before actually earning them through years of experience. I thrived with this freedom, and it gave me space for hours of solitude wandering through the woods, dreaming and imagining high up in the branches of trees, and having my bare feet and hands in intimate communion with the natural and wild realm, sharing appreciation and receiving wisdom from this vast and brilliant web of life that is our Earth. Now, I get to share Rumi's adventures and the wild grace of this love story with you, and I bow in reverence for the beautiful opportunity to connect heart-to-heart and soul-to-soul as we journey together in this realm of compassionate co-creation and evolutionary miracle-making.

Soul Nourishment

How can you praise and celebrate yourself simply for existing? Placing a hand on your heart, ask yourself what your most tender parts need to hear in order to feel affirmed and loved. Take some space to journal about what these spaces and places would most appreciate hearing from you. Explore writing affirmation statements honoring these precious parts of you and putting them somewhere you can see them every day for a lunar cycle, like on your bathroom mirror or on your altar. Even a daily "I love you exactly as you are" can work wonders in healing some of the most vulnerable parts of ourselves that have felt judged or unaccepted, and as we heal and whole internally, we begin radiating this wholeness and loving kindness to the world around us.

CHAPTER 3: INTENTION

"Look inside. Everything you want, you already are."
~Rumi

One of the most beautiful gifts from my journey with Rumi has been the invitation to an even greater awareness of the power of intention. When she came home with me that first magical day, she came laden with a bag of medications, a thick stack of documents detailing her medical history, and a long list of restrictions and cautions. When my veterinarian met with her the following week, she was astounded at the intensity of Rumi's medications at such a young age. She gently encouraged me not to expect Rumi to function like other dogs, noting that Rumi might never be able to go on a long hike with me or savor some of the activities other dogs engage in.

Now, four years after that initial homecoming, she's the fastest dog in the forest. Admirers marvel in awe when she zooms through the woods, slaloming through the trees like an all-star agility queen (which she is), leaping over fallen trees, and dashing up and down cliffs at the speed of light. It may sound like I'm exaggerating, but I'm not; it's truly phenomenal to witness her power and prowess, and people often remark that they didn't realize she only has three legs because she's so graceful and strong in her movement. Sometimes, I just stop and watch in wonder, my heart overflowing with gratitude at witnessing her joy and confidence and also feeling my overwhelming appreciation for her seemingly miraculous healing and transformation into a world-class athlete. At first, I used to find myself in a mix of cringing fear and fervent prayer as I would witness her crashing headlong down the cliffs towering over the creek bed, racing after an offending squirrel, or flying helter-skelter down steeply forested hillsides after deer. Now, I've witnessed enough times the way her paws always land in the right spot, how she magically always takes the right track, zigzagging through trees and over boulders at a speed I can't fathom moving myself, her body always landing safely and catapulting her to the next leaping bound. It would be remarkable to behold anyone soaring with such grace and speed over such wild and varied topography with no path and ever-changing terrain, but to witness a being who is short one leg and who has overcome so much is truly awe-inspiring.

I'm sharing this because I love celebrating how amazing she is and because she continues to affirm the power of intention, belief, and action to shape our reality. When we combine inspired awareness with focused love and care, miracles happen. From the first day she arrived home, still full of stitches and unable to let her heart rate get even slightly elevated, we've been affirming her strength, wholeness, and well-being in every way, and she's lived that into reality. The first night we fell asleep together, I remember whispering affirmations of her power and perfection into her soft little ears while she slept; over and over, I would tell her (and I still do) how amazing and strong and well she is. It's become a mantra for us throughout the day, reminding her that she's the best dog on the planet, so strong, healthy, and kind. Since our first morning together, we've begun every day singing her songs, "Every single cell in my body is happy, every single cell in my body is well," along with "Thank you for this dog, spirit, thank you for this dog, this wonderful, this wonderful, this wonderful dog." I've only been away from her two mornings out of all of our years together, and on those mornings, I sang to her in my heart, knowing she was hearing me and devotedly weaving those intentions and energies into her new day. Rumi's entrance into my life has amplified my intentionality, not only in being aware of my thoughts about her wellness but also about how each moment of our day influences and shapes our experience. To some extent, I was already practicing this on my own, but not nearly as much as I do now because of my commitment to her happiness and well-being. Most of our days are intentional, from waking up with songs, devotions, and cuddles to prioritizing time to pause and play and honor what would bring her joy, to maintaining a routine that's supportive of her wellness and ending the day with love, affirmations, and healing touch. We can do this for ourselves, each other, and our planet with every thought and every word, creating an evolutionary miracle tomorrow with the intention and gratitude we breathe and believe into today.

In so many ways, Rumi has invited me into a better version of myself. One of the most notable is how she's fine-tuned my awareness of our ability to positively influence reality with what we choose to believe. In that initial moment of realizing the extent of her injuries, the unexpected lengthiness of her recovery, and the possible lifetime of limitations, I felt a rush of doubt. And then I dropped to my knees, and our eyes met in one of the deepest moments of soul connection I'd ever experienced; instantly, I was aware of the power we were being offered to change the course of her life for the better. Still gazing into each other's eyes, all doubts dissolved in the light of my faith in her complete recovery as I felt us silently committing to a new story. From that moment, the miracles I've witnessed in her have shattered any limited thinking I might have had about the incredible ability we all have to heal, and about the power we have to positively influence the healing of another. Her shaved, emaciated little body has grown into the gorgeous jaguar-esque little Adonis that she is, her muscles rippling through her luscious, velvety black fur and her glowing smile and clear, shining eyes radiating a confidence and a strength that could move mountains. The power we have to believe ourselves and our world into a healed, whole, and radiant state of being is real, and it's just waiting for us to claim it as our path of conscious co-creation. If it feels good, I'd love to invite you to pause and envision the Earth and all of life as healthy, thriving, and abundantly well in every way, with lush mountains and meadows, clean flowing rivers and oceans, and harmonious ecosystems, breathing light into that scene. Next, you could envision all of your relationships thriving, centered in loving kindness and mutual adoration, breathing light into that vision. And finally, you could see yourself in glowing well-being, breathing light into that reality and noticing how you feel. If it feels appropriate, give thanks in advance for the tomorrow that you've just helped to create.

Consciousness is a living field of energy that is affected by what we think and feel and how we direct our attention.

The Hawaiian term *makia*, "energy flows where attention goes," illustrates how the unseen creative force of the Universe goes wherever we focus our awareness. This concept is supported by many other wisdom traditions and by current research in quantum physics. *Manawa* is a Hawaiian term that often translates to "the moment of power is now." Together, makia and manawa illustrate the potency of directing our focus in the present moment to channel energy toward positive outcomes. This brings me back to the power of our breath to intentionally open our consciousness to the larger divinity present within and all around us in every moment. For me, this often begins with slowing down the breath and intentionally creating space between the thoughts to soften mental patterns. Meditative practices help us develop the skill of directing our attention and maintaining focus. I sense that our evolution into the Symbiocene Era, one that is guided by a commitment to harmony and care for all beings, will involve a global consciousness shift in which we can maintain focus on the divinity connecting us all while also honoring our individual soul paths. This shift will birth something new and amazing because of the expanded perceptual capacity to be a unique whole within a harmonious constellation of other unique souls. Rumi invites me into this awareness every day, as her character is so strong and individuated from mine. She clearly and boldly lets me know her preferences and desires, yet also mirrors how we're living and creating together as one, two beings who are part of a greater, gorgeous web of existence.

Living in the forest, with no pavement and very few humans for miles around, invites us even more deeply into interbeingness as we're immersed in an ocean of other living beings, whether they're trees, birds, or blades of grass. Each time I step out the door or look out the window, I'm aware of the countless more-than-human beings with whom I share every breath. The trees, birds, and honeybees know how to live with harmony as their guiding light, and the consciousness they offer in every moment is one rooted in benevolence. They're inviting us back into right relationship with all of creation, which is why time spent in nature is so healing. Not only does it heal in the way it calms the nervous system, but it also heals in how it helps us remember who we truly are and why we're here. As we step more fully into the Age of Aquarius, we're releasing the outworn conditioning of the Age of Aries that was carried over into the Age of Pisces and developed into power-over systems of domination and oppression that resulted in unconscious living.

This fear-based thinking hasn't colored the more-than-human realm, and their steady presence in kindness is helping us remember how to choose a more intentional way of living. It starts with connecting from the heart, which our beloved companion animals and plants help us practice every day. As our hearts open, we can receive the love around us, which elevates and alchemizes us into wiser, kinder, higher-vibrational souls. As we do so, we begin radiating that energy out, and as *like attracts like*, we join the collective awakening and global consciousness shift into harmony. This is how the transformation into the new age happens, one choice at a time, each individual having the good of the whole guiding their intentions and actions, which then creates that reality for all.

Life force and consciousness are one. We know that we can shape reality by directing our intentions; we can believe each other and our world into miracles. I know this first-hand from witnessing my own healing after a severe car wreck at age eighteen that left me unable to walk, talk, and use my brain in ways that most of my peers could at that stage of life. Despite doctors' dire predictions about my recovery, or lack thereof, more than two decades later, I've healed in ways I couldn't have imagined, hiking on steep terrain for miles a day, my mind clearer and more capable than ever, and my voice strong and powerful. The source behind this miraculous healing? My mother's committed intention and belief. Whenever I've talked with her about how I got from the ICU to where I am now, she always says the same thing, "I just didn't believe them. I knew you were going to be fine." She simply didn't accept the medical opinions that I wouldn't fully recover, that my brain was permanently damaged, or I wouldn't ever be able to walk again. The power of this kind of belief is extraordinary. How we see someone or something can greatly influence their reality, and we can shape all of existence through breathing loving intentions into this vast and infinite web of consciousness that's creating us all in every moment.

The other day, I was supporting a companion in her healing journey, and she asked me what allowed me to believe in my own recovery after my car wreck when there were no external indicators that I would be okay. I shared about the blessing of my mother's belief in my healing, yet my companion pressed me about what inside of me had let me believe in this possibility. What came forth was a beautiful conversation about faith. Faith is often defined as complete trust or confidence in someone or something. While I may not have always had *complete* confidence that I would recover so fully, a flame of faith was alive in me that was always present, even amid supposed setbacks or unexpected challenges as I navigated my healing journey.

> *In the Pali language, the language of the original Buddhist texts, the concept of faith translates from saddhā, which means "to place the heart upon."*

Saddhā means to give our hearts over to something in that sacred way that can only happen with trust in something greater that will carry us from one state of being to a new and better version of existence. I remember that first day when Rumi arrived home, and I realized the enormity of her injuries; I felt an edge of fear, a hint of worry, maybe even a whisper of doubt in my ability to steward her into complete healing and wholeness. And instantly, something so deep inside me that it felt like it came from beyond me dissolved that fear, and I had the experience of saddhā, of placing my heart upon the love that would ultimately heal and transform her into thriving beyond our wildest dreams. It was a sense of saddhā because I knew I couldn't do it alone; that feeling of placing my heart, my hope, upon this sacred space of grace is what invited in the unseen support and guidance that I needed to care for her in that first year. Little by little, she grew stronger and more able, and I began to see far beyond the limitations her doctors had predicted.

I had a similar experience in my healing journey when, after a month in the hospital, I arrived at my parents' home to continue my recovery. Finally free of the distractions of painkillers and the medical environment, I was able to fully comprehend the extent of my injuries. I remember waking up that first morning and feeling almost unable to believe what had happened, overwhelmed with the reality of not being able to walk and incredulous at the face looking back at me from the mirror, so swollen and covered with stitches that I barely recognized myself, my teeth covered in a gridwork of wire holding my broken jaw in place. I felt tears beginning to well up in my eyes, and then I felt Spike's silky fur as he came in closer, his warm body anchoring me into a reality far beyond the overwhelm I had felt closing in. I felt us both take a breath together, and a softness flooded my being. In that moment, I felt him inviting me into the frequency of saddhā as we both gently placed our hearts together on the altar of faith. I can't even say that I had total belief or confidence in the journey before me, but in that moment, something shifted inside me in a way that I was no longer focusing on all that was broken in me; instead, I was noticing the small miracles that were occurring in and around me. Spike was mirroring something to me; his faith in me, like my mother's, was enormous, and even if mine felt wobbly at first, their reflections nurtured mine into an all-powerful commitment to my full resurrection. As I share this, I feel tears flowing as I remember the beauty of his profound love. If it feels good, I'd love to invite you to savor a deep breath with me, pausing to honor all of those who have loved us into being through their unwavering faith in us and their devotion to our care. May all beings give and receive this frequency of love.

Christianity highlights that all one needs is a mere speck of faith, as tiny as a mustard seed, to nurture and sustain the miracle-creating force that's always present and ever-available to us along our evolutionary journey. Do we have faith in our ability as a collective to evolve in ways that allow us to live harmoniously and come up with new ways of seeing and acting together that inspire care and love beyond all the false narratives of separation? I have so much more than a mustard seed of faith in our capability as a species, as a planet, to self-actualize into the love we came here to be, and I have faith in our ability to nurture and encourage each other in our individual remembrance of how to embody in these ways. Am I willing to give my heart to this vision and commit my life to doing the work necessary to transform my conditioning and patterns in ways that will serve this dream of a just world? I am. When I pause and feel the faith alive in me, I can sense how at one time, my faith might have been closer to seed size, yet now, as I write this beneath the steady hum of cicadas on the second-to-last day of summer, I feel saddhā infusing every cell of my being. I feel it overflowing from within me, radiating through the energetic layers around my body, infusing the warm air, and merging with the faith emanating from the trees, birds, and light surrounding me. It invites me to embrace the beautiful new path being illuminated before us.

In many ways, I feel that saddhā goes hand in hand with gratitude, creating a sacred alchemy that becomes the elixir for the manifestation of our dreams and visions. We're likely all aware of the power of gratitude to soothe the nervous system and redirect our thoughts in a positive direction, yet I hadn't thought of gratitude as a way to actually co-create with the larger forces of the Universe until I lived in Hawai'i. The axiom for my *halau*, sacred school in Hawaiian, is *ho'o upu upu*, which translates to "grace receiving gratitude." What this reflects is that we don't quite know what comes first, the grace that arrives that evokes our gratitude or the gratitude we gave in advance for the grace we knew was on the way. The teaching was that when ancient Hawaiians were out on the vast ocean with no land in sight, they would offer this prayer, giving thanks in advance for the appearance of land, and inevitably, a shoreline would appear. The invitation is to give thanks in advance, even when we don't have any outward evidence that something has actualized, knowing that the gratitude we're offering is helping the vision to manifest because of the frequency it creates in our hearts, thus magnetizing what we desire more effectively. Many studies have shown how focusing on gratitude generates healing in the body and elevates levels of the feel-good hormones that help bring us into greater states of alignment. Like a domino effect, this then begins to draw in more positive experiences to us, creating more gratitude, and the beautiful spiral continues. This is why, even when things seem to be falling apart, finding even one small thing to have gratitude for can shift the energy so that it can turn the tide, and as previous distress fades into the background, we can move forward.

When Rumi was first recovering with me, not only did we sing our song of gratitude throughout the day, but I also offered gratitude for the smallest accomplishments in her healing. As I did, I witnessed more and more of them showing up. We had what at the time felt like some major setbacks or challenges in her recovery. Yet, each one allowed us to redirect our energy to gratitude and shift our energies to align with the vision of her complete wellness. To this day, it seems almost impossible that I've recovered to the extent that I have, and Rumi's vet continues to marvel at how she has surpassed expectations of what she could achieve in this lifetime. Not only are Rumi and I both incredibly strong, healthy, and able, we're flourishing in mind, body, and spirit, and we're sharing the blessings of our journeys with those around us. We're all way-showers on this planet. What are you mirroring to those in your life? How can you expand your awareness of your potential and that of those around you? How can you be the one who believes a miracle into being for yourself or our world?

Ike is Hawaiian for "the world is as you see it" or "you create your own reality." This love story is an invitation to create with your awareness and let it lift you into a new state of consciousness where more options are available for living from gratitude, connection, and wonder. This awareness creates space for new creative forms to become available in our consciousness and opens new avenues for our evolutionary journey. What can emerge from this space is a global awakening to who we really are and what we're here for, a collective homecoming led by a collective messiah. It's all possible because, as the Hawaiian term *kala* illuminates, the Universe is limitless, and that infinitude is alive within you. It's all a practice; go gently with yourself, focus on the positive aspects in any moment, and watch your world transform. Our focus is everything, it's reality-shifting. Love what you love. The first step is turning toward that which opens your heart. In that way, we are *pono*, Hawaiian for living righteously and being in perfect alignment with the Universe.

> *When we're in right relationship with the truth of our souls,*
> *we're always in harmony with all of creation.*

We can enhance this co-creative potential by listening from our souls to the souls of others, which often happens in sacred silence. There is deep healing in being in silence with another, and many of us often experience this blessing with our more-than-human companions, savoring the rich nourishment of resting in quiet together. How you see anything is how you see everything. Can you see yourself as whole, perfect, and complete, exactly as you are? Can you feel yourself loved just for that? Try extending that to the entire world and feel your heart expand. It's about attuning to a new frequency, which is subtle and simple. It happens when we soften and come into our bodies more fully, breathing from the heart field and redirecting our awareness to flow to and from the heart of the Universe.

We can place our sense of security in the eternal love and infinite generosity that this divine consciousness has to share with us, and in so doing, we become a new humanity and a new Earth.

Soul Nourishment

Placing a hand on your heart and breathing deeply into your core, ask yourself what qualities you would most love to embody and radiate to the world around you. Take some time to journal about each one, inviting yourself to dream about what action steps, small or large, you might take to nurture these qualities within yourself. As you feel yourself mirroring these energies to those in your life, how do you see your life and those of your loved ones being enhanced? In what ways could you expand your awareness of your own potential and that of those around you? If you were going to believe a miracle into being for yourself or our world, what would that look and feel like for you? Take some time to breathe deeply and listen within before taking space to journal about any visions that came through.

CHAPTER 4: TREES

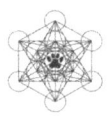

"Love is the whole thing. We are only pieces."
~Rumi

Basil, my first three-legged love, is buried right outside our sanctuary, his bones laid lovingly in the earth at the foot of a towering grandmother oak. The entire area around the tree has become an altar to his spirit, with a smooth, flat rock to rest upon and gorgeous redbuds circling the space, showering lilac-hued petals over the land in the spring. It's a portal of grace, with rose quartz and turtle shells outlining his resting place, prayer flags blowing gently above, and bright green moss creating a welcome carpet at the base of the tree. His presence is palpable, and I witnessed Rumi's communion with him for the first time right after we moved in. It was nearing sunset, and I didn't see her in any of her usual spots. Right as I was about to whistle for her, a flash of light caught my eye, and I looked over to see her sitting transfixed at the foot of Basil's oak, her paws planted reverently on the soil directly over his body. She had a stillness I rarely observe in her; her head tilted back as she gazed up into the branches and out toward the distant setting Sun simultaneously. I watched silently as she sat purposefully until the Sun slowly disappeared behind the ridgeline and then touched her nose to the base of the oak before heading toward the cabin.

The next day, I found her there, this time with her little back snuggled in against the tree's broad trunk, sitting silently with intention and an almost enraptured presence, her paws planted on the marbled roots spreading slowly out across the mossy earth. I felt my inhalation reach deep into my heart as I sensed the energetic sharing happening: Rumi was held by the oak, her paws radiating love down into the ground, where Basil's bones nourished the tree's roots with grace and beauty. In a single breath, I got a glimpse of the often-unseen magic that is the glorious exchange of love happening all the time amongst our more-than-human kindred. This cooperative intelligence enables our existence, much like the brilliance of billions of interconnected tree roots sharing resources beneath the soil. This network allows forests to thrive, creating clean air for us to breathe and offering countless other wild blessings to our living world.

I breathed in wonder as I beheld Rumi with Basil's tree, aware of the surge of life force energy pulsing in the divinity of that moment, which is in every moment, every living thing, and every sacred exchange of presence between beings.

When we pause long enough to be present to this aliveness radiating in the plants and living beings around us, a doorway opens for something exquisite, and an alchemical beauty results from this exchange of divine intelligence.

The pure, raw wisdom of the natural world is a beacon in this time of radical transition, and the trees are some of our greatest teachers. Every conversation I've ever had with the tree world has been profound and healing. I believe all the brilliance they've shared with me over the years can be summed up in one wise and gentle invitation: "Open your heart."

The energy exchange between Rumi, Basil, and the oak is tangible every time I see her out there; the love of Basil has infused the roots of the oak, and Rumi graciously receives and contributes to this sacred collaboration as she sits in prayerful presence. My heart still melts every time I behold her in this sweet and silent reverence, though it's become so common that it feels like it's part of her regular routine. I understand this sacred connection, as most of my life has been guided by the grace and wisdom of our tree kindred. Growing up, I spent countless hours amongst the trees, climbing them, resting in their welcoming arms, swinging upside down from their branches, creating with their leaves and bark, and delightedly building treehouses in our backyard's glorious patch of woods. When home life felt tumultuous, I would climb into the treehouse I had built, and it felt like I was in another world, one that was eternally caring and safe, an ever-welcoming and ever-loving presence that felt like a true home. The awareness of trees as sacred guardians and trusted friends was a foundational part of my life growing up. I could always count on climbing into one or resting my hands or back on a welcoming trunk to anchor me in whatever way I might need. However, it wasn't until I was in my early adult years that I fully recognized the power of the tree-human connection.

I had just graduated from college and taken on the somewhat overwhelming job of directing a nonprofit organization while also navigating the recent ending of a relationship. I felt a deep longing for support, to be truly held and connected, yet I didn't know where to turn for it. I was walking in the woods, one of my favorite ways to process my emotions, and I was deep in my feelings when a silent voice said to me clearly and kindly, "Let me hold you." Without a second thought, I was drawn to the gorgeous maple tree at the edge of the forest meadow as I felt her beckon me up into her outstretched branches. As I laid my hands on her rough bark and started climbing, I felt her draw me into her welcoming lap, her wide arms opening around me and holding me high off the ground in a near-perfect nest of support. As I leaned my spine against one of her broad branches, I felt my whole being soften, opening like a flower as my system relaxed into a sense of connection and safety deeper than anything I'd ever experienced with another human.

In that moment, a gateway of awareness opened, a door flew open where I didn't even know one existed.

My heart opened to receive the love offered by this beautiful, satiny-leaved giant creature of grace. It was a moment of inner jaw-dropping as I felt my swirling emotions and bodily tensions dissolving in the embrace of this steady care. It was a mental, emotional, and physical awakening to the power of communion that trees offer us all the time. I felt her sturdiness, full presence, and total ability to hold me with such tenderness that my most vulnerable places could finally relax and feel loved. She held me in a way another human wouldn't have been able to; she showed me what's available in the more-than-human realm of care when we open to the supreme wisdom and grace always on offer.

I've been a tree hugger since I was little, yet it wasn't until adulthood that I began to notice trees calling me to them and pulling me into their embrace. Now, it's simply a part of life; I'll be hiking and suddenly feel the energy of a particular tree calling me over, my outstretched arms gratefully encircling its trunk while I sense its energy wrapping me in kindness and inviting me to pause, rest, and breathe together. After years of living in this beautiful forest, I have particular trees that I stop and connect with most days, feeling our mutual appreciation of one another and our shared awareness of the gift of exchanging these sweet moments of adoration. One of my favorite ways to connect with the tree realm, and one of their favorite ways to connect with us, I'm convinced, is to hike or move in a way that raises my heart rate and then stop and lay my heart upon their trunk, heartbeat to heartbeat, allowing our aliveness to nourish each other while witnessing the alchemy in our shared presence and physical affection. Sometimes, I like to put both hands on a tree and imagine my energy and love flowing from my right hand out into the tree, with my left hand opening to receive the love shared by the tree—a reciprocal circle of appreciation that permanently transforms us both. Every time, I sense the trees loving the feeling of our shared aliveness through this intimacy. As they receive the energy flowing from my heart and draw it deep down into their root systems, I feel them sharing it with the network of roots of all the surrounding trees, and I witness the upwelling of gratitude in the forest all around me. I like imagining all the trees worldwide feeling our love as I breathe with them in silent grace. In these moments, I hear the song of the trees, an ancient and emergent melody that feels like it's calling me home, deeper into myself and deeper into the embrace of the sacred universal kinship we share with all of creation.

Living in this forest paradise allows me the blessing of hearing this woodland symphony evolve with the seasons and beholding the depth and richness of how we're all growing together as one family, being guided by the natural evolutionary cycles. One of my most treasured experiences in spring is hearing the budding leaves on the treetops begin to make their first music with the breeze. The gentle song of the newly birthing canopy, after months of silence in the beautiful bare-branched window of winter, never fails to nourish my soul with exhilaration and awe-struck wonder. The first rain that arrives on this nascent green rooftop brings yet another dimension of reverence as the drops sound their enchanting canticle on the new life high above, the canopy gratefully drinking it in and alchemizing it into aliveness.

Equally as delicious is when late summer arrives, and the trees begin humming a new tune, their once-soft green leaves beginning the journey of morphing into a dazzling rainbow of colors as they slowly start letting go, and the forest becomes filled with the rustle of the breeze wafting through their drying forms. It's familiar, yet it's new every time; the scent in the air changes as the lush green womb around us begins to slowly thin out, sunlight pouring through in new places as glimpses of the distant horizon start appearing in the freshly opened spaces. Every year, I have the same two responses: delight in the shift toward fall—one of my favorite times of year—and, concurrently, a little bit of sadness at the idea of letting go of the lushness of summer and the joys it brings.

This is just one of the many ways that trees are brilliant teachers. They model the art of letting go with grace and continue to remind us of the peace that comes with allowing the natural spiral of life to flow without trying to hang on to something once its time has come. It's a wonderful mirror for me to look at whenever I may feel hesitancy around change due to being comfortable with the way things are, which often happens for me at the beginning of autumn. By late September, we've settled into a summer rhythm, the long barefoot days and abundant gardens offering a sense of fullness that feels emotionally and physically nourishing. While I often think of autumn and winter as my favorite seasons here, there's a sense of outward companionship that I feel from the warm hug of the humid air and the green aliveness all around that I feel resistant to let go of when the season begins to shift. When I listen more deeply within, I notice a tenderhearted wondering, not quite a worry, not exactly a fear, more of a heightened awareness of the mystery inherent in change. As much as I celebrate the inward pull that autumn and winter invite, that rich, deep dive into the inner fertility of winter's womb and the creative alchemy that it offers, the truth is that I don't know what's coming. Some part of me wants to hang on to the known companionship of summer's heat and fullness.

This is why the initial change in the forest's love song as the leaves crunch underfoot invites me to deeper intentionality. It's the harvest time of releasing what's no longer needed and gathering what will carry us through until spring. So now, as I write while watching the first golden leaves begin to drift down toward the earth, I ask myself what I'm afraid of. The answer that floats up from my depths is loneliness. I breathe into that, as lonely is a word or feeling I would rarely use to describe my experience. I know that I'm never alone; I'm with the divine always, with my angels, and with all of the loved ones I connect with throughout the day, and all of those points of connection need not fade due to the seasonal shift. Yet there's a more profound sense of the invitation being offered in these yin seasons of the year, the times of autumn and winter when the natural world is more attuned to the inward, feminine aspects of life. In autumn, there's an invitation to let go of our metaphorical leaves from the past summer to make way for the inner alchemy on the horizon. As I write now, I look up into the cool, clear sunlight and offer my prayer for this dawning season of fertile reimagining. Humbly, I whisper, "I want to be so present in our communion, Divine, that I feel your love flowing through me in the holy river of remembrance of who I truly am, always." A gentle breeze wafts through the tall cedars around me, whispering, "It is already so, Beloved. Smile, and give thanks." I do.

We moved to the forest in the middle of winter, the woods bare and open, the sunlight spilling through the windows in bright bands of rose gold, bathing the sanctuary in a cozy, welcoming glow. How we celebrated the gift of that warming light as the temperatures plummeted and the snow began to arrive, piling into the house after frozen rambles through the woods to be nurtured in the sunlit haven. Sitting in front of the west-facing windows as the days turned toward dusk, we reveled in the expansiveness of seeing for miles out into the forested valley and feeling the last rays of sunlight on our skin and fur. It was a bit of a shock when spring began to turn to summer, and we were suddenly surrounded by thick walls of green towering above us in every direction. The long-range views disappeared, as did the sunlight pouring in through all the windows and doors. However, as spring ripened into summer, the cool shade of the trees and the soft, diffused green light brought enormous relief and delight, keeping us cool and allowing us to be outside almost any time of day without being in the blaze of direct sunlight. That is a tremendous gift for someone who enjoys spending about eighty percent of their waking hours outside. It's all so miraculous, really. The way the natural world works to care for and support us in the ever-changing seasons and weathers of life is something worth celebrating every day. I love wondering about all the ways the natural realm is nourishing us that we're not even aware of. I intend to open my senses to perceive more of these invisible blessings, giving thanks in advance for the grace of this quiet, generous benevolence.

One of the greatest blessings I sense from our tree kindred is the way they're helping us remember how to consciously communicate from the heart. Have you ever walked into the woods and immediately felt your energy shift in a positive way? It happens to me every time, especially if I return to our woods after being in a more urban area. As soon as I step out of the car, I feel a wave of peace and gratitude engulf my entire being, and while I'm always struck by the beauty and quietude surrounding me, what truly sweeps me off my feet is the energy of love I feel emanating from the wildness around me. In addition to savoring the beauty I feel receiving this energy, I most appreciate how it gently brings my awareness down into my heart, where I feel a river of gratitude pouring forth. I feel myself soften into what feels like my true self. This self feels anchored in a quiet inner calm, and I sense a deep and eternal sense of connectedness within myself and all of life in the Universe.

This heart opening that the trees invite is an experience of something much vaster than our minds can even begin to grasp, welling up from within and embracing us from all around, lifting us into a state of grace.

It can be so soft, quietly coming in like a whisper from the soul, or it can come in like a love tsunami, exploding delight in every molecule of our beings and bringing us into rapture with all that is.

It vibrates beyond the confines of language, and because of that, it requires a surrender, a radical openness to the mystery, to not knowing and to believing in something much greater and more powerful than our minds can begin to comprehend. I take such comfort in this awareness of the larger benevolence that's always present because it offers a reprieve from needing to know the way forward or to have it all figured out. We're not supposed to know; we evolve by remembering that we're part of a great mystery we're here to learn from and with.

The natural realm communicates from this field of awareness in ways that sometimes our mental understanding can't quite grasp, which is why living from and directing consciousness into the heart helps us to receive and integrate this higher wisdom. As we attune to that awareness, something extraordinary begins to happen. As I write, I look up and take in the green all around me, miles of thick forest surrounding me on all sides. It's like being submerged in the *anahata*. Anahata, Sanskrit for heart chakra, translates to "unstruck sound," suggesting that our heart field contains such purity that it is whole in and of itself. To me, that suggests that even amid all the external influences that can alter our minds or bodies, we have within us an untouchable and incorruptible wellspring of love that is always guiding us, that is always available as a source of sacred nourishment and connection with the grace that's ever-present.

This source of love is alive and active.

It's a consciousness that's growing and evolving in and through us. It requires our participation, and we can choose to say yes to it, to allow ourselves to become aware of being breathed by love itself. When we turn our awareness toward this miracle within, it invites us into another dimension of collaboration and engages our brains in the vibrational field of the heart. This allows our perceptions to shift so that the world we birth through the stories we tell becomes one rooted in harmony. According to researchers at the HeartMath Institute, the human heart has an electromagnetic field more than five thousand times more potent than the human brain, which indicates that if we can shift to thinking from the heart, we can even more potently influence our reality to create a new paradigm oriented in this frequency of love.

Biomancy is the energy exchange between biofields and the study of the magic that happens in these exchanges. It is an avenue for exploring this synergistic creation happening all around us all the time.

There's something new being birthed in every moment.

As I write, I look over to the stately Sycamore, reaching her smooth limbs out toward me. I offer her words of my deep appreciation, and as I do, I feel her gratitude rippling back toward me through the air between us as I hear her say, "It's all vibrational." We're vibrational beings, and when we're living from our hearts, we communicate from that frequency, which magnetizes more of that to us. As we learn to be more conscious of the vibrations we're emanating, we can translate the new light being communicated to us in vibrational waves from the trees and other green plants around us. These new photonic light codes bring fresh nourishment to our hearts for the awakening of dormant DNA strands, activating new genetic codes of potential to remember our divinity and embody this frequency of grace. Where our attention goes, energy flows; when we allow awareness to drop from the head into the heart as our tree family continually invites us to do, we begin to embody love itself more fully, coming into harmony with all of creation as a living, breathing field of divinity in form. Exploring the potency of this reciprocal relating by allowing ourselves to slow down enough to hear the song of the natural world is enough to completely transform our understanding of who we are and why we're here. I invite you to gift yourself the space to pause and breathe into the energy of the trees at dawn and dusk, opening your heart to their sacred offerings and giving thanks for the incredible insights and blessings you receive.

There's a new and ancient way of being alive emerging on the planet; it's a sharing of wisdom across morphogenetic fields, the fields of energy and consciousness that guide and shape like-minded systems into creation. A harmonization of previously "separate" energies is happening, and the Vesica Pisces is a beautiful illustration of this phenomenon. The Vesica Pisces is a visual image of two circles overlapping and creating a third circle in the middle that brings forth a new creation from the alchemy of the original two. I've witnessed how the opening of our minds and hearts to the intelligence of the more-than-human world creates a divine alchemy in our beings and in the morphogenetic field or shared consciousness of all of humanity that can bring forth a new, evolved state of awareness that inspires a more cooperative landscape for all of life.

There are many ways to connect and co-create with the natural realm; for me, the first step in that direction is simply opening up to it. With open minds and hearts, we're free to create new meaning from our experiences; our descriptions of life shape the way we experience it and build the future we're living into. It isn't just a restructuring of the old; we're living into an entirely new paradigm.

Softening our grip on previous ideas of how the world works can open gateways of brilliance as space for new possibilities is offered.

In some ways, we're working with a new medium as new light codes stream onto the planet and upgrade our internal operating systems in ways we likely can't even begin to fathom. Much of our current understanding of the natural world is based on a classification system of separation. While I understand the original reasoning behind this, I wonder what it would be like to create a lexicon of relatedness based not on separation but on connection. All beings—rivers, stones, trees, cats, humans, stars, air, ancestors, and elementals—carry an energy signature based on a shared vibratory intelligence that is the source of all wisdom and an invitation for collaboration. These connections and conversations, rooted in reverence for our interbeingness, will guide us forward in birthing a new and more harmonious existence for all beings.

Soul Nourishment

Is there something in your life that feels ready to be released? Perhaps it's an outdated belief, a worn-out self-definition, or a limitation on what could be possible for you in this lifetime. Explore connecting with a tree by placing both hands on the trunk and feeling the flow of energy in through your left hand and out through your right hand, sensing into your own roots reaching down into the Earth along with the tree's roots. Feel the power of your grounded energy as you bring to mind that which is ready for release. Allow the tree to support you in practicing letting go, breathing deeply as you create fresh new space for that which you're ready to welcome into your world. Explore leaning your back against the tree or leaning in with your heart on the tree as you allow yourself to feel the peace that comes from allowing the natural cycles of letting go to happen with grace. Breathing, simply allow yourself to be held by these sacred, wise ones as you witness the power of your own faith and presence in communion with that of the trees.

CHAPTER 5: WINGED ONES

"You have wings. Learn to use them and fly."
~Rumi

The day was just beginning to dawn, a hint of sunrise glowing on the horizon. I walked outside, the steam from my mug rising in the early morning air, and inhaled deeply the sweet scent of cedar and pine, the soft earth cradling my bare feet. The inner smile had already reached my lips as I inhaled more fully, reveling in the holy marriage of savoring and surrendering, when their song floated through the still-waking forest air. I felt it sweep me off my feet, my heart opening to another dimension of love, my mouth smiling even wider in awe as I beheld the graceful burst of blue arcing through the air. As this language of light filled the space, the notes opening new fractals of awareness in my atoms, time stopped and leapt in a single moment. I felt the brilliant melody playing through the lyre of my being, each note ringing deeper in my bones as it flowed in crystalline clarity through the soft morning light.

Rumi and I stood silently, smiling in wonder, breathing in the blessings, and wordlessly offering our wholehearted gratitude for the experience. I've been captivated by bluebirds for most of my life, their song and form resonating with my soul on a deep level, and the kinship I feel with them has been a gateway for connection with the other miraculous winged ones with whom we share this planet. I've often felt that birds are angels. How could they not be? They sing gorgeous songs all day long, soar gracefully through the skies, and live in exquisitely crafted homes nestled in the branches of trees while generously offering healing music and beauty to the world, asking nothing in return. Attuning my awareness to their wisdom and grace has opened my heart in profound and magical ways.

My appreciation for our avian relatives took on a new depth when I first heard bird feet dancing on the roof, which is now one of my favorite sounds. Even just thinking about the sound, I feel a smile spreading across my lips, my heart softening with love as I sense the pitter-patter of robin feet tapping out their rhythm as a new day dawns. In our previous home, I would hear them in the kitchen, the one part of the house where the roof was such that their dance steps could be appreciated, and my entire being would melt in delight, my heart overflowing with gratitude and awe for the grace of such intimacy. Did they know I was bowing in wonder as they tap-danced above me, silly with smiles as I paused my kitchen projects to marvel at the miracle of their Morse code of sweetness? Why does even the memory of it elicit such awe in me? Because it's so extraordinary, even in its complete ordinariness. The majesty of sharing such moments of beauty with other precious ones—ones so supposedly different from me, winged ones a fraction of my size who sustain off bugs and worms and soar through the air—brought a connection of such pure love that our differences faded as their tiny dancing feet translated into a deep communion of adoration in my consciousness.

In some ways, these moments of connection touch my soul more deeply than hours of heartfelt verbal soul-sharing with other humans. Not that one is better than another; it simply bears noting that there's a language of the natural realm that can alter us in profound ways and open us to new depths of awe that can transform us in miraculous ways.

This opening, this transformation, is one that I feel is key to the emergence of the new and more harmonious world we're here to birth.

The wisdom being shared from the more-than-human realm might come in like bird feet dancing on the roof rather than through a straightforward equation or formula for action, as the wisdom is of a heart-opening nature that transcends linear ways of knowing. These moments of connection that fill us with wonder recalibrate us to a vibration of beauty, kindness, and care, and the more we open ourselves to experience them, the more we magnetize them into our reality.

My spiritual connection with birds began evolving when I first communed with one of my greatest more-than-human guides, the red-tailed hawk. I was in my early twenties, balancing living in an urban place with many long hikes in the nearby woods that graced the area. I wasn't sure what bird it was, but it communicated with me so intently and directly that my attention was riveted. I watched in reverence as it soared above me in what seemed like deliberate, purposeful circles. I breathed in wonder as it swooped and glided, its wings riding the breeze like a skilled surfer savoring the sweetest wave. I watched in awe as it circled twice and then floated down beside me, close enough to look me in the eye and for me to behold the majesty of its auburn-colored tail feathers. In one life-changing, heart-opening moment, our souls connected, and then it was gone, gliding swiftly through the forest and out of sight. Slightly breathless, I offered a silent thank you as I paused to integrate the depth of connection I had felt in the clarity of our communion. As I turned to go, I looked down to see a single perfect feather glowing with aliveness on the pine-needle-covered trail. It was the first of many, many hawk feathers that would grace my way, each one a clear sign that I was on the right path and right where I needed to be, even, and especially if it came amid various emotional turmoils or periods of uncertainty. Every time, my spirit breathed a sigh of relief and exhaled a prayer of gratitude for the confirmation of the divine support always beside me, encouraging me on my journey.

Hawks inspire a feeling of rapture in me, reminding me of the wisdom that lies beyond our ordinary ways of knowing. When I'm present with them, I often feel a sense of being contacted from beyond the three-dimensional world in a way designed to expand my perspective and open my heart. One late summer afternoon, they flew high above as I floated in Iris, our forest lake oasis. Looking up at the deep blue sky, my eyes fell on a tiny figure soaring high above, so high I could barely follow its long, sloping arcs through the air. As my vision was drawn to another, soaring even higher above, I wondered about how they were seeing me and was reminded of the power of our perspective, to be able to pull back, to see the expanded view, and to witness how everything is touching, connecting, and creating together in any moment. As the sunlight reflected on the pine trees and a snake glided silently by, making barely a ripple on the clear, calm surface, I felt my awe and admiration for those two-winged angels above me, and I knew they were receiving my appreciation. The invisible current of grace that gave them the courage to fly so high in the sky was the same grace that carried me on the clear surface of the water and saturated my heart with the beauty floating high above me in the endless blue.

Hawk wisdom helps me remember to soften my focus, expand my perception, and open my awareness to higher ways of perceiving. They inspire in me the joy of surrendering my established truths about myself and the world, opening me to a more beautiful reality that unites me with the heartbeat of all creation.

As I type, the owls call back and forth through the warm evening summer air. I chime in occasionally; they're lovingly tolerant of my amateur hooting, sometimes throwing me a bone and hooting back in my direction. It was when I was living in Hawai'i in my early thirties that I first encountered the depth of owl medicine. *Pueo,* Hawaiian for owl, is often regarded as an *amakua,* a sign of the ancestors. My whole body would fill with the presence of something greater when they flew by me in the softness of the night, their wings whispering peacefully through the warm jungle air. Entranced with their magic, I began praying to them when evening began to fall, feeling them calling me closer as I opened my awareness to the wisdom they carried in their silent grace. Then, one late winter afternoon, I stepped into the home of a gentle medicine woman, and she greeted me with sacred sage while fanning me with the largest pueo wing I had ever seen. My inhalation instinctually deepened as the wing's powerful energy opened a spaciousness around my body that brought a sense of supreme safety and presence. Sensing my appreciation, she quietly placed the wing in my hand.

Instantly, I felt my whole body enliven with the wild beauty emanating from this sacred treasure of creation.

Soon after, I was heading out for an early morning hike when I encountered a newly fallen owl in the middle of my path. Observing that her spirit was free from her body, I offered prayers for her life. I reverently carried her home to bless the next chapter of her journey by ritualizing her wings so that her medicine could continue its work. Hours later, her wings were curing in a sacred bath of cornmeal on an altar adorned with crystals and rose petals, where they would rest in graceful transformation for the next two months. Now, many years later, these sacred wings grace our sanctuary altar and offer exquisite healing and illumination to all who are blessed to encounter their power. These holy-winged relatives have such wisdom to share.

One of my other beloved aviary allies is the holy hummingbird. In addition to their exquisite beauty and enchanting vibrational grace, hummingbirds are also a physical wonder. They have the highest metabolic rate of any animal on Earth, as their hearts can beat at over a thousand beats per minute, and even though they have an exceptionally high need for oxygen, some species have adapted to live in the high-altitude and low-oxygen ecosystem of the Andes Mountains, thriving at fifteen thousand feet above sea level. This seeming miracle is possible due to a small genetic mutation that occurred in the process of metabolization of oxygen in their blood. This quiet inner alchemy has allowed these magical creatures to flourish in previously uninhabitable areas. It's also allowed these high-elevation environments to integrate the medicine of these tiny way-showers, resulting in more diverse and varied ecosystems and cultural expansion. This evolutionary shift offers divine inspiration for the possibilities of our own transformations that could allow us to thrive and coexist in new and previously unimagined ways. What if a tiny change, perhaps catalyzed by the sonic frequencies being shared through the birdsongs at dawn or through the exchange of love between my heart and yours as you're reading this, could lead to a subtle transmutation in our physiology that allows us to awaken to our sacred interconnectedness and remember what we came here for? Perhaps we could also begin breathing in new ways, flourishing in new spaces, and co-creating more cooperative and varied landscapes that are mutually beneficial for all of life on Earth.

Related to my awe of our avian kindred is my most frequently recurring dream: flying like a bird. It's almost always the same in that it's the miraculous experience of having my feet on the ground and being anchored in one reality, then moving my arms/wings to ascend into the air and take flight. The exhilaration and joy of it is extraordinary and always finds me in wondrous delight upon waking. The dream begins with an inspiration to move my arms, and after a moment or two, I start to lift off the ground as an unseen force carries me high into the air, where I'm soon soaring with complete ease and grace. I once heard that our arms resemble the osseous material that comprises birds' wings. Could it then be that we have the inborn awareness of taking flight, and could this imaginal impulse guide us into the remembrance of flying in a new and previously unimagined way?

Perhaps our taking flight might not be an actual experience of flying but a capacity for mobility and connection that could allow us to be alive together in profound new ways.

Just as the hummingbirds in the Andes Mountains experienced a tiny genetic shift that allowed them to thrive in previously uninhabitable areas, we, too, can open to and nurture emergent transformational possibilities by softening our previous limitations around what it means to be human.

An ancient teaching offers that humility and courage are the two wings we need to fly through the skies of life. I love this because it invites us to be humble in the vastness of what we don't yet know while also being courageous enough to surrender our preconceived ideas of reality in order to be open to the great mystery of existence. I like to practice this with my breath, intending to release all I've known on the exhale and bring in the fresh new potential on the inhale. It always expands my perception and leaves me smiling.

The birdsong at dawn reminds me daily of the vast potential that's always being offered to us, the way the gentle notes float down through the trees, ever new in their tones and frequencies, each time attuning me to the grace of the new possibilities glimmering in the emerging light. It's at dawn that I can most often sense the attunement happening in the birdsongs, as I feel the harmonics activating new subtle awarenesses in my mind through the vibrations entering my auditory field. It reminds me to pause my thoughts, inhale more fully, and acknowledge the greater divinity alive in the holy serenade of these winged teachers. The variety of melodies and the sheer number of voices creating them in concert in the forest is mesmerizing, especially in the spring and summer months.

The more I learn to slow down and receive the blessings being offered, the more I'm acutely aware that the music of nature is profoundly guiding us in our ascension journey. These more-than-human way-showers are tuning our fields to higher dimensions of harmony, elevating our cellular consciousness through a transmission of grace carried on the sound current and integrated through our own process of presence with this divinity. This nurtures a remembrance in the fabric of our being of what harmony feels like as we allow it to penetrate our awareness and inform our manifestation. It doesn't require any cognitive processing; it asks only that we be open vessels for the beauty being shared, embracing our own sacredness through the embodiment of this wild harmony and mirroring it back to all we encounter.

Adding to the beauty of these beloved harmonizers is their oft-reverenced ability to show up as communication from the ancestral realm. This has been true in my life and is acknowledged in many ancient traditions. Throughout my life, my grandmothers have shown up very clearly as cardinals and woodpeckers, often appearing in ways so obviously conveying their presence that it's left me laughing out loud. The drumbeat of the woodpeckers that reverberates through the forest valley in early spring always brings me into conversation with my grandmother, who was bedeviled by the woodpeckers that would peck on the side of her wooden house. To deter them, she hung up pie pans, shaking her fist and delightfully dialoguing with them when they began pecking, hoping to send them on their way. Additionally, when a dear friend was in her final days and knew that her earthly journey was coming to a close, she told me she would appear to me as a hawk. Shortly after she dropped her body, I was hiking through the tall pines, speaking to her memory in my heart, when a gorgeous red-tailed hawk flew low and slow beside me on the trail, floating through the air alongside me as I breathed in wonder and spoke aloud my love. There was no doubt that it was her, and I felt us both smiling from head to toe when she finally let a soft current lift her as she soared gracefully into the setting Sun. Then, a few weeks later, during a moment of powerful communication with a grandfather who died before I was born, a giant owl came swooping out of the trees, flying so incredibly close that its huge wing created a breeze over my body that

I felt deep in my bones. Bowing and smiling, I gave thanks. These sacred beings invite us into a new paradigm of praise, where we communicate through tones and rhythms of beauty, inspiring each other to embrace the divinity around us. Together, we lift our mighty wings of courage and humility, opening ourselves to the mystery of a new way of coexisting and embodying harmony. I could share volumes about my awe for these dear ones—the crows, bluejays, redwing blackbirds, summer tanagers, sparrows, wrens, and all the others—yet I will conclude by simply inviting the opening of mind and heart more deeply to the sweet medicine of these sacred teachers, allowing their heavenly *icaros*—sacred, shamanic songs—to penetrate our molecules and uplift us in the embrace of their vibrational grace.

Another brilliant and beloved winged one is the dragonfly, which spends much of its life underwater as a pale predatory larva. Then one day, it crawls out of the water on a twig or a branch and quickly mutates into the iridescent rainbow creature we know as a dragonfly. The genetics of a dragonfly are already within the larva while it swims around underwater; it just hasn't activated them yet.

This is a beautiful metaphor for the paradigm shift we're in as a species and as a whole. Our planet can no longer support a paradigm based on exploitation and domination, and the genius of nature is guiding us to get curious about what's possible if we let go of what's no longer working and get creative about what could come next. This is the brilliance of the natural realm; it's always curious about what's coming next and opening to what's possible for creating systems of greater harmony. When we shift our attention from focusing on what's falling away to getting curious about what's possible, we activate new codes of potential for how we might evolve.

The pressure of the stress that we're going through as a planet is creating a dynamic tension within all of us that has the capacity to produce new life, new expressions of aliveness that work better for our planet as a whole.

In this moment, new potential is buried in our biology that's just waiting to emerge.

Like the dragonfly, the genetics are already there for a new and improved version of humanity, and they can be activated with our awakened imagination and belief in the possibility of a new world. Like the dragonfly, we're going to become the new and better version that's coded inside of us, just waiting to be born.

What's coming is different from what many can currently conceive of and is inviting a profound activation of the creative imagination as the new consciousness dormant within us comes alive and ushers us into a new reality.

How can we get curious about what's possible?

How can we direct our awareness to imagine new ways of being human and more-than-human together? May our avian kindred inspire us to look toward new horizons, to allow our wings to be lifted by the morning breeze, to let the medicine of their song penetrate deep into our cellular consciousness to awaken new ways of knowing and expanded ways of creating harmoniously together. May they inspire a manaʻoʻio, a faith, in us as great as the hawk soars, as wise as the owl sees, and as beautiful as the bluebird's song.

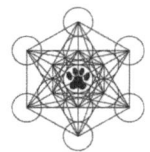

Soul Nourishment

How can you invite your imagination to expand its edges, to open and receive new inspiration and dream beyond its previous horizons? Explore sitting outside and allowing all of your attention to turn towards the beauty of the birdsong around you, inviting it to penetrate deep into your cells and influence your consciousness with its tones of wisdom and grace. How can you allow yourself to evolve in ways that allow you to more fully embody your own unique soul song in greater harmony with all of creation? What dreams within you are longing to take flight, and how can you invite yourself to begin spreading your wings in ways that will support the manifestation of these sacred visions? If it feels good, explore offering your own birdsong back to the winged ones around you, noticing how it feels in your body to communicate in tones and melodies that may be new to your experience. Do you notice the birds singing back to you? How does the rest of the ecosystem around you respond to your offering? When we intend to communicate beauty to the world around us, miracles happen within and without. Take space to simply listen, notice, and give thanks.

CHAPTER 6: FLOWERS

"Speak a new language so that the world will be a new world."
~Rumi

Rumi loves flowers. She's the only dog I've ever known who stops and purposefully smells her blooms, gazing intently into the blossoms as she inhales and sometimes closes her eyes as she breathes in the scent, an energy of deep reverence emanating from her whole body as she savors the experience. I noticed her appreciation of flowers at the beginning of our first summer together, when a beloved rose bush had just begun to open, its luscious deep-red petals opening in pillows of beauty and radiating a rich and delicious scent, a whisper of clove with a hint of citrus nestled into the rose sweetness. I had gone out to pick one, and after taking a few deep, long whiffs of her magnificence, I looked down to see Rumi looking up at me expectantly. I offered the bloom to her, and she leaned in, inhaling deeply with her eyes closed, then exhaling in a long sigh of appreciation and satisfaction.

Now, when I pick roses, I know to share them with her waiting nose, and I delight in feeling her full-body response to their healing energies. I love to pick them in the morning when they're fresh with dew and put them where we'll pass by them throughout the day, stopping to inhale their grace when walking by, then moving them to the bedside in the evening so that their scent can infuse our dreams while we sleep. I've always loved roses. Some of my sweetest gardening memories are of helping my mother in her garden and being enchanted with the intoxicating scent of her roses and their mysterious beauty, layer upon layer of gorgeous petals opening in a perfect spiral of evolution, each one offering up another wave of ambrosial scent and captivating grace. So when the first roses began opening soon after bringing Rumi home, I was delighted to discover our shared appreciation of these floral allies. Does she truly love the smell of roses? I don't know; she doesn't respond to them with the same enthusiasm that she does to, say, a piece of salmon skin. Yet she clearly appreciates them, and I often catch her pausing to sniff other flowers with a sense of wonder and presence that I've never witnessed in another dog.

The first time I planted rose bushes in the forest came after dreaming of growing roses for years. I lovingly purchased three amazing plants that I placed in the ground with reverent love, envisioning months of blooms filling the woods with their delicious scent and offering exquisite beauty for years to come. Covered in buds, they quickly produced gorgeous blossoms and then immediately stopped creating new growth and became riddled with various rose diseases that were likely the result of living in a densely forested area with many bugs and limited sunlight. I spent countless hours trying to remedy their problems with all the natural solutions I could come up with, but my sweet roses didn't flower anymore for the rest of the season. The following year, having learned more about growing them, I met their springtime greening with what they'd needed, all along to be well-fed. Now, I feed them generously every week with the organic rose food they love, and I have gorgeous roses in all seasons other than winter when they're in happy hibernation. They remind me to be even more conscious of what stories and energies I'm feeding myself and the world around me and to keep feeding the creative vision of a thriving planet in a way that will keep the metaphorical roses of my dreams strong enough that they can thrive even amidst the challenges of living in the forest of our current reality.

What are the stories you've been feeding yourself about thriving and belonging?

Perhaps they're ready for an upgrade in order to weave a new narrative that reflects your—and our—infinite potential to cultivate a global garden thriving with beauty and radiant wellness for all beings.

Embracing our evolutionary shift is about attuning to a new frequency of cooperation that will feed a new story of interconnectedness in our world. Flowers help me with this in the ways they, like trees, redirect my awareness to the heart. Something about their quiet beauty and infinitely generous offering of grace instantly softens me back into that orientation within my own being. When we're rooted in our hearts, it completely shifts our perspectives, opening up new possibilities for solutions and harmonious paths that may have been invisible when seen from a more cognitive orientation. The natural cycles of their evolutionary spiral model this exquisitely, from leaf to bud to flower, and then to the drying and decaying that allows a new cycle to take birth the following season. If we, too, remain flexible, open, and adaptable, we can flow with the larger cycles of transformation, and we can breathe with the inevitable changes of life rather than getting caught in trying to resist them.

We can fuel a story of disaster and "problems" or feed a vision of evolutionary creativity wherein we embrace our roles as conscious co-creators in a newly emerging world.

In addition to feeding the dreams that align with the kind of world we want to live in, we can also be flexible with how they might come to fruition. In this way, we create space for the miracles that naturally show up when we're open to something better arriving. I experienced this when I tried planting grass around the cabin after moving in. I diligently sowed the best organic grass seed I could find, selecting a variety specifically created to grow in the forested conditions of our homestead. Months went by and nary a blade came up, the packed clay soil too dense even for grass to grow. I went to plan B, which was to spread smooth river rock on all four sides, creating a wide parameter all around that was a beautiful alternative to the wet mud and offered great sunbathing options for Rumi.

Every day, I would happily look out on the glowing stones, deeply grateful for this much better option than grass, as it needed no care and created a much-welcomed, bug-free zone around the cabin. A year later, as summer began to deepen, I noticed some curious little plants growing up through the stones. In awe, I watched as hundreds of *salvia coccinea*, or hummingbird sage, began making their way out into the world, bejeweling the river rock with gorgeous nectar-rich stalks of the cardinal red flowers that are a beacon for hummingbirds, bees, butterflies, and other local pollinators. I had planted some in the flower bed at the edge of the river rock, and the breeze had gracefully spread their seeds out into our rocky little yard. Not only was it more beautiful than anything I could have ever envisioned, as I wouldn't have thought anything could grow through the depth of the rocks (or in the clay soil), but we now have a yard filled with a gorgeous sea of fragrant ruby red blossoms and delighted hummingbirds and butterflies savoring the nourishment.

How can we be more open to new possibilities and unexpected blessings that show up when we release attachment to how we thought something should be?

When we soften our awareness to receive the sweet wisdom of the floral realm, we open ourselves to new dimensions of beauty and grace that can shape our evolutionary awakening in the most magical ways.

Speaking of magic, borage is one of my favorite flowers for inspiring this opening to the wild blessings of the floral world; this pink-blue star-shaped herb of gladness is revered as a natural mood lifter, blooming prolifically with little care and offering all aerial parts for edible and medicinal enjoyment. I remember the first time I encountered one; it was love at first sight. I felt a deep kinship that I knew would last for lifetimes and likely had existed in many lifetimes prior. The more I learned about this amazing flower, the deeper the connection I felt with it, and once I started growing borage myself, I knew we were in it for life. Why am I so enamored with this little purple-and-blue wonder? I love all the elements she offers—her healing energies, beauty, and fortitude—yet it's something deeper than that. Flowers and plants carry unique signatures and vibratory frequencies, which are part of the power of flower essences as sources of healing medicine. When I speak of vibration concerning plants, stones, water, or any other more-than-human energy, I'm speaking of the *prana* carried by that energetic field. The prana is the living essence carried in the medium of the consciousness, whether it be floral or human or other. This *pranic* energy affects us all, though not everyone chooses to turn their attention toward it so that they're consciously engaging with it in a collaborative way. When we do, new potentials for wellness emerge that we may have never imagined possible.

Flowers offer vibrational nourishment and healing, the frequency of which is empowering, affirming, and magnetic to miracles. It is an energy imbued with beauty and grace, which helps us translate the crystalline codes of awakening carried by these floral allies into our consciousness.

Flower essences are a form of plant medicine that work at the vibrational level to treat the cause of the disease and alleviate the symptoms. This is possible because of the multidimensional intelligence carried by the floral realm. Roses, yarrow, calendula, violets—all flowers have a unique vibrational signature that can help shift unhealthy patterns to help elevate us into states of more vibrant well-being and energetic harmony. We're always speaking energetically, and when we remember how to live from the heart-centered frequency that flowers and our other more-than-human kindred invite us into, everything changes within and around us. As more of us begin living from this space, a groundswell of energy builds that becomes contagious, similar to the hundredth-monkey effect. Once enough of us have evolved, humanity can instantaneously shift into living from this higher vibration powered by our collective awareness. The more-than-human realm is helping us to remember how to live from this heart-centered orientation, and as we connect with this energy, we begin embodying that state more fully.

Living from the heart allows us to process mental information through a filter of loving kindness and a connection to the divine.

This shift enables the mind to serve the heart, leading our actions to focus on the greater good rather than ego-driven, separation-based intentions. The natural realm helps us remember what our ancestors understood: we are all eternally connected to a field of love that permeates all life on Earth. This field provides infinite nourishment when we open ourselves to receive its grace.

My mother is one of my greatest teachers in life and my inspiration for opening to the wisdom of the floral realm. It's been a beautiful journey to witness her sacred relationship with plants and flowers, as she was the one who first nurtured my connection with them. After countless days joyously helping in her sprawling garden as I was growing up, I eventually became the one to tend to them as she matured in years and became unable to do so herself. Similarly, I took over the care of her huge collection of orchids that she had been tending for years, which gave us the shared joy of delighting in the magic when one suddenly burst forth in bloom after months of hibernation. In her journey of cognitive evolution, her deepening delight in flowers—in the vibrancy of their colors, their companionship, the sunlight on their leaves—has been one of the greatest gifts of being beside her as she progresses in the later chapters of her earthly journey. She often notes that the flowers are "sparkling," her voice conveying a sense of reverence and wonder at the depth and richness of what she can behold. Every time, it commands me more fully into the present moment, making me stop to marvel with her at the latest bloom and let my vision and mind soften so that I, too, can behold the heightened beauty that she's perceiving. Her enhanced ability to attune to this depth of magic and allow it to elevate her spirit reflects deep wisdom. I bow in wonder to this sacred weaving of intelligence between the floral realm and our blossoming hearts.

This divine intelligence of the flower world is most apparent when I witness how flowers evolve in the shifting seasons and the insight that illuminates my evolutionary journey. I love deadheading flowers and removing the spent blooms so that the plant can channel energy into new growth—it challenges me to look at my own resistance to change. There's such beauty in the dying blossoms, yet at some point, the pollinators and plants will benefit from their sweet release. The natural world helps me remember the power of letting go in the death cycle that becomes a gorgeous midwife for the new growth to come. A delicious experience of this was going out to the garden this morning and witnessing a luscious lion's mane mushroom growing on the fallen oak log that I'd used to create an herb bed. This limb that had seemingly died was now birthing sacred nourishment and medicine, which it would likely produce for years to come. How can we learn from this wild wisdom and repurpose our fallen limbs, the parts we may deem broken, so that healthy, new life can emerge?

A frequent opportunity to explore this is presented to me when I notice limiting beliefs or patterns and realize I can let them compost into fertile space for a new and better perspective to emerge. A welcoming way to see beyond any limiting perspective is to ask myself, who would I be without that outworn belief? Remembering the exquisite beauty and nourishment that springs forth after deadheading the Mexican sunflowers always inspires me to attune to the alchemical power of letting go. For me, it starts with the intention and usually involves calling in support from my guides and helpers to clear out what no longer works if I'm still holding on to it. Sometimes, our *vrittis*—the Sanskrit term for the mental grooves formed by repeatedly thinking the same limiting thoughts—require us to consciously replace them with more aligned visions. Mindfulness practices can help loosen these stuck energies. Our personal and collective outdated thoughts can be transformed into new, more positive iterations as nature continually adapts. In autumn, fallen leaves and spent gardens decay and break down, enriching the soil for the next growing season and providing a habitat for tiny organisms that deeply nourish the Earth. Year after year, trees and plants release what is no longer needed, and beautiful new life emerges after the sacred rest of winter.

I love the invitation to my own conscious wintering—a rich and sacred time for introspection, gestation, and embracing the uncertainty of what will emerge. As I write, we're about to head into the portal of winter, and I feel a deep sense of relief knowing that the quietude I feel within is precisely where I need to be. I have a palpable sense of something old dying away and not yet knowing exactly what will take its place. Amid all the other feelings that might stir up, I have faith in surrendering to the mystery through witnessing the natural world's graceful embrace of the season. Faith and patience are essential to our evolutionary adventure, and the datura flowers were a supreme teacher for me in this aspect this summer. I lovingly planted their seeds in the spring, carefully transplanting the seedlings into the garden weeks later. I watched devotedly as the vines wove along the garden fence, trailing gracefully and forming stunning buds as the days lengthened. However, then it seemed as if nothing was happening. There were no openings, no blossoming, and I wondered if something had gone awry.

As I was writing on the front porch one late July morning, my gaze was suddenly drawn up the hillside to the diamond-white glow of not one but two gorgeous datura blooms shimmering from the garden. In awed delight, I made my way to their side, marveling at their mesmerizing sacred geometric beauty and intoxicating scent. Burying my face in their soft petals, I inhaled deeply.

I felt something smiling deep in my core: the eternal faith and patience whose steady anchor within allows for some of the most miraculous blossomings in my life.

Since then, whenever I'm feeling impatient or thinking that something isn't going to happen, I inhale deeply and recall breathing in the wild beauty of that first datura. When we have the courage to let go and let faith be alive in the unknown, we're unlimited in our capacity to create and be created.

Another wonderful teacher in this practice of patience and faith is garlic. If you are a garlic fan, perhaps you love the wide palette of flavors in the different varieties or its exceptional medicinal and therapeutic benefits. I love all of those, though the thing that enchants me the most about this plant is how miraculously it grows. Every season, I'm in awe of how I pull cloves from the bulb, tuck them lovingly into the soil, and then, despite giving them little to no attention, nine months later, I harvest an armload of beautiful specimens that provide us with almost a year's worth of medicine, with plenty to share with loved ones. I also love the romance of harvesting it, which was enhanced this year by the Full Moon on the horizon.

We went out after dinner as the Sun was slowly setting on the first night of summer. There was a hum of aliveness in the air and vibrant greenery all around. Barefoot in the golden light, I loosened the soil around the tall green stalks and gently lifted the rose-colored bulbs from the earth, carefully brushing the soil from their skins in preparation to cure. Rumi helped diligently until she became too sleepy to be an active part of the process, digging a little bed for herself in the leaves so she could monitor my progress while in repose. Eventually, as the last of the sunlight faded softly into the horizon, she sleepily made her way down to her bed on the front porch to doze while I finished up and carried the fragrant armloads down to the cabin.

The scent of freshly harvested garlic on an early summer night is soul-healing.

As I laid each one out to dry, my gratitude overflowed at the magnitude of nourishment these humble globes would offer us over the coming months. I would set aside the largest bulbs to plant back in the ground in the fall, allowing a new generation of garlic to grow from these select few. The generosity and ingenuity of the plant world are astounding, guiding us to embody this vast wisdom and resourcefulness in inspiring ways.

Chapter 6: Flowers

Flowers and plants invite us to speak a new language, one that's vibrational and relational. This field of connection and communion is one based in love, in rich hues and textures and intoxicating scents that can shift our consciousness, in patterns of beauty alchemized from the living light of the Sun, and in the healing nourishment they offer to our minds, bodies, and spirits. Plants have imagination; they translate light and water into healing frequencies. The astounding array of forms and colors that flowers offer to the world transcends explanation: the floral queendom seems like proof that an all-loving and wildly creative intelligence is guiding us all. Add to that the incredible scents from our floral allies, and there's no denying that this Earth is infused with a magnificent and benevolent divinity.

There is also the miracle of perennial flowers and the seasonal blooming of bushes and trees, with forests and meadows exploding in color and scent year after year. These natural events nourish pollinators and fill the world with joy, perfectly aligning with each season's cycle. Have you ever paused under a blossoming mimosa tree and brought your face close enough to feel the magic of its silky tendrils caressing your skin, inhaling its enchanting sweetness? Or stood beneath a blooming redbud and eaten the sweet-tart purple flowers straight from the branch or gathered handfuls of violets to scatter across the top of pancakes? Have you beheld an echinacea opening, the flowers starting as soft green nests, opening miraculously into the firm pincushions of nectar so treasured by our native pollinators? The shade of purple from the opening echinacea petals is in and of itself amazing, and the vibration of its color elevates my consciousness every time I stop to witness its majesty.

This blossoming of consciousness being inspired by our more-than-human guides reminds us of how we're all part of the web of awareness, sculpting reality in every moment through our thoughts, words, and actions. It's a vibrational field that we can positively influence with every expression of gratitude we offer to the world, supporting us to embody more heart-centered lives. One way I love to connect with the floral realm is to introduce myself to a flower or plant and truly share my heart and most vulnerable and tender parts in a way that allows me to develop a relationship with the plant. It allows me to come into a true kinship with this more-than-human friend to open myself to the wisdom and healing it offers.

The more we practice forging this intimacy with the natural world, the more we build our capacity to communicate and co-create with these brilliant teachers.

A gentle way to explore this kinship is through breath and intention; flowers of all kinds are wonderful allies in this practice. Either with a flower in front of me or imagining one, as I inhale, I intend to fully receive the blessing of its scent, exhaling fully and deeply in gratitude for the vibrational nourishment. Sometimes, I expand this practice by breathing in an infinity loop from the center of my heart as it circulates up around my head and back down around my feet, encompassing my entire being in a field of heart-centered energy that resembles the auric field of a flower, radiating beauty in all directions.

The sensorial nourishment offered by our floral allies is allowing our transforming awareness to be grounded in a more somatic awareness of the beauty that's guiding us into a new paradigm of existence, and this gives us a greater capacity to be in energetic alignment with that which is best for ourselves and all of creation. This morning, the Sun was just beginning to rise, and I saw the first rays of light glinting off the velvety body of a beautiful black spider who had woven a stunning web through the sunflowers. I watched in awe as webbing flowed swiftly out of her abdomen from a seemingly infinite store of silken grace. She neatly wrapped a newly caught fly in her web. The rainbow luminescence of her web in the rising sunlight as the breeze rippled through was nearly as mesmerizing as witnessing the supreme focus of her inspired vision to securely wrap her future feast. In that moment, I was invited to surrender to what's happening that's so much bigger than what I think might be happening, to open myself even more fully to the miracle of the rainbow web that we're all weaving together as we let our mana (internal power) flow forth toward the inspired vision of the sustainable future we're here to birth.

Our consciousness is being reshaped, we are restorying our world, and our more-than-human kindred are lighting the way with the sacred beauty they continuously model for us on the evolutionary journey.

May we learn to embody this grace and reflect it to all those with whom we share this brilliant garden of life.

Chapter 6: Flowers

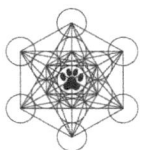

Soul Nourishment

Find a flower you feel drawn to and create space to take several deep breaths with this floral ally, turning your full attention to its form, scent, and energy. As you breathe in conscious connection, invite yourself to fully receive the blessing of its vibration, opening your heart to the blessing of its scent and the grace of its beauty. You can expand your connection by breathing in an infinity loop from the center of your heart up around your head and back down through the heart and around your feet, enfolding your whole being in a field of heart-centered energy similar to the auric field of a flower. Breathing here, allow the beauty of your own vibration to radiate out in all directions. If it feels comfortable, now would be a wonderful time to silently or aloud share any concerns of your heart, and with your journal, write down any communications that you receive back. When you feel complete, thank the flower and, placing a hand on your heart, offer gratitude and loving kindness to yourself.

CHAPTER 7: THE COSMOS

*"The Universe is not outside of you. Look inside yourself.
Everything you want, you are already that."*
~Rumi

It was late summer, and I had just emerged from the cool quiet of the cabin into the bright heat of midday. Glancing over, I spotted Rumi lying on the hot river stones, panting, the strong Sun radiating off her black fur. I laid my hand on her head and felt it pulsing with heat; instantly, I knew she was charging herself with the powerful sunlight pouring down and reflecting off the stones. I looked up at the golden orb high in the sky and felt myself drawn to lie down with her to absorb the energies being offered. The stones were practically sizzling, and the air was thick with heat, yet it felt profoundly soothing. We lay together, immersed in the transmission that was happening, breathing deeply until I felt a distinct shift in my ecosystem, almost as if something had clicked into a new, higher alignment.

At that exact moment, Rumi gave a big stretch, yawned impressively, and got up to go back inside, her sunlit activation process complete. More and more, I notice that on certain days, there's something irresistible drawing me to soak in the rays of the Sun, even if it's blazingly hot and seemingly the last thing I might want to do. And when I started tracking the solar activity, the emissions from our Sun that send powerful blasts of energy to the Earth's atmosphere like flares, plasma influxes, and coronal mass ejections, I noticed that Rumi would most often be out there on those high-energy days, soaking in the new photonic codes despite the intense heat. I took a cue from her, and now, when I see her out there, I often go and soak in them with her; she's like a little barometer for cosmic blessings. Similarly, she's exquisitely attuned to the cycles of the Moon. On New Moon nights, she's much more inward and cuddlier, often going to bed early and sleeping in later than usual. On Full Moon evenings, she tends to be more energized and livelier, directly reflecting the energies of the Moon. The forest mirrors this innate wisdom, with the owls and coyotes becoming much more vocal and active during times near the Full Moon and a deep quiet and stillness permeating the valley on nights when the Moon is invisible. By paying attention to the movements of the stars and planets, we can attune ourselves to the greater song of the Universe. This cosmic guidance helps us navigate the global changes driven by this galactic field of loving consciousness.

This greater song is the *musica universalis*, or harmony of the spheres, which expresses the exquisitely orchestrated movements of the celestial bodies—the Sun, Moon, and planets—as a form of music. Originating in Pythagorean times, it fused mathematics, music, and astronomy to create a theory that these planetary movements created a form of music that can be heard by the soul and that influences our lives in profound ways. Because of the perfection of the celestial world, this music is always harmonious. While it might not appear to be audible to our physical ears, its presence is constant. It supports the evolution of embodying our integrity to become more aligned with universal harmony. Because we're all vibrational beings, we're energy vibrating in relation to the energies within and around us. We're constantly emitting a frequency, and according to the theory of morphic resonance, we attract energies that reflect the frequency we're emanating. Thus, when we attune our awareness toward the harmony in the heavens—whether through studying astrological happenings, bathing in the sunlight and moonlight, tending our gardens according to the lunar rhythms of the planting calendar, or intentionally communing with these more-than-human celestial way-showers—we have the opportunity to consciously shift our vibration to come into greater harmony with this universal symphony of love.

We're constantly emitting our own music; our own notes are being played in the song of existence.

Chapter 7: The Cosmos

We're made of sound and light, and the celestial bodies are inviting us to receive the light they radiate as a way to come into a new dimension of embodiment that allows us to be part of this greater harmony in new and extraordinary ways. There's so much support being offered; all we need to do is look to the sky, open our hearts to receive, and give thanks as we witness our transformation in the grace of this cosmic intelligence guiding our way.

We're held and guided by the consciousness of the cosmos, as there are energies at work supporting us that are beyond human comprehension. We're in a timeline shift connected to the processional cycles of the planets and stars, and there are new codes of awareness coming in through the sunlight, moonlight, and starlight. The space between cycles, as in the shift of ages we're currently navigating, contains great fertility and richness, like the space between breaths.

Right now, the space we're in contains vast potential for us to evolve as a species and as a global energy in a direction of increasing cooperation and kindness.

As I write this, we're approaching solar maximum. This happens regularly, about every eleven years, when the Sun grows increasingly active and is tracked by the amount of sunspots on the Sun's surface. These sunspots, some of which are as big as the Earth or larger, are created by the Sun's powerful shifting magnetic fields. During the peak of activity in the solar cycle, the Sun's magnetic poles flip; then the Sun begins quieting as it moves toward solar minimum. The increasing activity of the Sun is bringing shifts in consciousness to all of life on Earth, supporting our transformation from a separation-based awareness to one that holds both our uniqueness and our oneness, allowing for collaborative living in ways that might have seemed unfathomable until now. The more we open ourselves to this incredible blessing being bestowed upon us, the more fully we can access these gifts and integrate them into the new reality we're weaving as a creative collective.

We're always in communication with the Sun, as its light informs every aspect of our existence; however, we can more intentionally co-create with this brilliant source of aliveness in ways that invite even more conscious collaboration with its power and guide us in directing our evolutionary journey with even deeper awareness. As the Earth continues to receive the new photonic light being emitted from the Sun, we, and everything around us, are being transformed in our ability to hold more of this high-vibrational light. This light is expanding the consciousness of the Earth herself, as well as the capacity we have as a planetary whole to embody a new way of being by infusing our atmosphere with new light codes that carry information designed to turn on dormant DNA and activate new genes in our bodies and the bodies of all life on the planet.

Fusion is the solar process that creates the heat and light we witness coming from the Sun, and it naturally occurs when two atoms are compressed and heated to the extent that their nuclei merge into a new element. This often creates photons, the particles of light released from the Sun, which result from the atoms deep within the Sun's core melting together and generating light. We take in this light all the time, whether through direct contact on the skin or the eyes or through the food and water we ingest, and we can enhance this alchemy by bringing greater awareness to the miracle that's happening every time we engage in these ways.

> *The light energy contained in a human cell is directly proportional to the intelligence that system can hold, and the light energy in human cells comes from the sunlight that becomes liberated from the food that's consumed when mitochondria interact with it.*

These mitochondrial bacteria break the double-carbon bonds in the glucose or fatty acid molecules that store the energy that the chlorophyll created to store the sunlight in these carbon bonds. All of the green plant world around us stores sunlight through double-carbon bonds, so the food we consume is a form of fatty acid or glucose that fills us with light. As we awaken more, we're increasingly drawn to foods that carry a high volume of light, as they nourish our inner luminosity and help us remember the light that we are.

In addition to consuming light through the food we eat, we can explore practices like Sun-gazing, in which one looks toward the Sun with eyes open or closed right at the beginning of sunrise or right before the Sun sets, and not more than for a few minutes right after sunrise or directly before sunset. However, listen to your inner wisdom; this practice may be more suitable for some than for others. Our eyes can be more sensitive to light at different times, influenced by the season and the stage of life we are in. Another way to invite collaboration is to talk to the Sun in whatever form and language feels aligned for you. I commune with the Sun daily, whether it's hidden by clouds or rain, either aloud or silently from my heart. I offer gratitude and prayers, inviting a conscious connection. Often, I pause during the day to look up and acknowledge the light as it moves across the sky. I love starting my mornings by looking at the rising Sun, inviting my heart to connect with the heart of the Universe through the central Sun, and I do the same thing at sunset, giving thanks for the day and welcoming the night.

In addition to sunlight, the light of the Moon is also powerfully healing and transformative. When we create space to receive moonlight on our skin, into our eyes, or by infusing water or other substances with its light and then drinking the charged water, we invite co-creation with this powerful lunar force, harmonizing our energy fields with its flow. The light of the Moon, *soma*, is a healing tonic for a culture that's overly focused on productivity and doing. The cooling and pacifying feminine nature of soma brings a much-needed balance to the fiery, action-oriented masculine emphasis on doing that's been prevalent in our recent history. Moonlight is the sunlight reflected off the surface of the Moon, so the powerful fiery solar energy is filtered through the cooling lens of the lunar forces.

In Vedic philosophy, soma is a nurturing, calming, mothering energy that can help restore balance to our overly masculine global climate. How exactly does moonlight influence our inner waters? In Vedic philosophy, soma represents all that is patient, sweet, delicate, beautiful, and gentle, and we can build this energy within by connecting with the Moon, water, and the beauty of nature. Soma is also known as cosmic plasma and is the subtlest form of matter. Physically, it's associated with the pineal gland and the neurotransmitter serotonin, which is why it's often associated with feelings of deep contentment, bliss, and nourishment.

When we invite ourselves into the receptive mode, we're more able to surrender into the grace of this energy, softening our edges and opening to something nurturing and welcoming for our whole self.

A mantra that can help build our connection with this lunar energy is *so ham*, pronounced "so hum." This translates to "I am that" or "I am pure awareness" and helps to connect our individual minds to the divine mind of the Universe. I like to breathe in "so" from my root to my crown and exhale "hum" from my crown to my root, repeating the sounds and the flow of energy as long as I desire, allowing it to calm my mind and bring me into even deeper embodied presence. If it feels supportive, I reverse the breath, inhaling from crown to root and exhaling back up, noticing the subtle shifts this brings into my embodied awareness. Mantra is often described as a way to purify the mind because it gives it a positive focus and distracts it from looping on unhelpful thoughts. This practice helps anchor our awareness into the greater energy of divine wisdom inherent in the lunar frequencies so that we can integrate the sacred cosmic nourishment on offer.

I've always had a special relationship with the Moon, as I came into the world in the middle of a history-making blizzard under the January full Wolf Moon. My amazing father braved the treacherous roads despite dire warnings for everyone to stay home, managing to get my ready-to-birth and equally amazing mother safely to the hospital. To this day, I have a visceral memory of seeing the full moonlight shining in the window soon after my arrival Earth-side, radiating a soothing sense of home into the new environs where I found myself. Now, when I go outside at night or before dawn and see her diamond-bright light illuminating the heavens, my entire being softens in a sense of deep inner peace. Perhaps we all have a special connection to this lunar source of grace, as she is the divine mother behind so much of our earthly existence, guiding the tides of our rivers, oceans, and inner emotional waters, informing the growing cycles of the plant world, and offering sacred nourishment for our spiritual, emotional, and physical well-being. If you've ever been hiking in a wild space at night under a Full Moon, you know the blessing of seeing the forest or jungle illuminated by the moonlight, the sacred way shown by this miraculous force almost 239,000 miles away from the Earth.

Saumya is a Sanskrit term used to describe a moon-like person, someone who's full of gentle inner beauty and light and radiates soothing, peaceful energy simply by being themselves. We can develop these qualities by intentionally connecting to the energies of the Moon and inviting these frequencies into our fields of consciousness through mantras, feeling the moonlight on our skin, charging our water and crystals with its light, or in any other ways that speak to us. We can then enhance the world around us by radiating these nurturing, calming feelings. When we invite more direct communion with this brilliant source of wisdom by charging our waters and crystals in its light, we allow their molecular structures to be upgraded, which we can then integrate into our field of awareness as we drink the water and engage with the crystals or other sacred objects. I love to lie outside when the Moon is full and let the light bathe my entire being, clearing my energy and nourishing me on deep, multidimensional levels. What we feed ourselves changes us, not just in what we watch on a screen or what we put in our mouths but in the light we intentionally take in at dawn or as the Moon rises, in the ways we speak lovingly to ourselves, and in how we direct our awareness. Mantras like "so hum" can be a nourishing gift to feed our consciousness, as they're a powerful tool to clear unhelpful patterns and direct the mind's focus to the Moon-like energies of peace and calm. An easy way to incorporate healing mantras into your world is to practice silently chanting them when you first awaken and when you go to bed at night, as these are times when the mind is in a powerfully receptive mode and can greatly benefit from the soothing energies of these vibrational remedies. Sometimes, when I'm breathing "so hum" during the night, I envision the Moon's gentle light surrounding me and filling every cell of my being with its grace, softening any tensions in my mind or body and inviting me into an even deeper space of presence and gratitude, which are the qualities I most often feel when beholding the vastness of the cosmos.

The miracle that life on Earth only exists because of the light we're receiving from a star over ninety-three million miles away from our planet, our Sun, inspires me with wonder. However, I find the incredible forces beyond our great central Sun influencing and shaping our existence even more awe-inspiring. Even greater in power than our Sun is the powerful energy pulling it toward the Galactic Center, the central region of our Milky Way galaxy. This area is home to a supermassive black hole that carries almost four million times the Sun's mass, known as Sagittarius A*. The Galactic Center's magnetic pull is pulling our galaxy toward it, while an even greater force known as the Great Attractor is pulling the Galactic Center toward it. This Great Attractor is the core of the Laniakea Supercluster, a supercluster of galaxies containing the Milky Way that exerts a powerful gravitational pull on all life in the Universe.

Lanikea is Hawaiian for "immeasurable heaven."

When I pause to breathe into this vision, I feel the potent energy deep in my core, pulling me into union with the immeasurable heaven alive in every particle of existence. There's a greater consciousness drawing all of life into its embrace, and it's the same consciousness that's alive in every cell of our beingness; it's the vast quietude and deep wisdom within that's helping us remember who we are and what we came here for.

Our biology and chemistry are being transformed by the new light coming in from the Sun and other cosmic sources of light intelligence in the Universe.

When we attune our awareness to connect intentionally with this wisdom, we can work with these powerful forces in profound ways. As Evolutionary Astrologer Heather Ensworth brilliantly describes, when we look back in time through the processional cycles, the twenty-four-thousand-year cycles that carry us through the energies of each constellation of the zodiac and influence how we view life, we can see now that we're in a time that ancient wisdom traditions have prophesied as a time of great remembering and awakening. The processional cycle takes us through a spiral of awakening, and we've come to a time in which we're receiving more intense energies from the Galactic Center that are supporting us in transforming physically, emotionally, and spiritually into a more highly evolved state of being. These energies are bringing up the trauma from our collective past that still needs tending so that we can heal and integrate it sustainably. This cosmic intelligence reveals that now is the time to remember our true selves, heal the illusions of separation, and establish right relationships within ourselves and with all of creation. Through healing our collective past, we remember the sacredness within ourselves and all of life, which becomes a gateway to a new era of existence.

The shift into the Symbiocene Era is guided by the wisdom of the natural realm embedded in the living Universe. When we look at the Earth's evolutionary process, we see that the species that have survived and thrived are the ones that have focused on living cooperatively. We're now remembering the power and beauty in this reality. As Black Elk of the Oglala Sioux tribe shared, "The first peace, which is the most important, is that which comes within the souls of people when they realize their relationship, their oneness, with the Universe and all its powers, and when they realize that at the center of the Universe dwells the Great Spirit and that this center is really everywhere, and within each of us." Our human potential is being facilitated by the intelligence of the natural world. We're witnessing the maturation of our species, and we're being gently led by the divine guidance in the trees, stars, and all the other more-than-human wise ones as we grow together toward a universal intention of harmony with all of creation.

There's a particular hum at dusk and dawn. It's a frequency and contains a deep wisdom that opens a window of awareness in our perception. It's the space between day and night, akin to the space between thoughts, that's a source of deep presence; when we attune to this space, incredible blessings are available. As we expand our consciousness to contain awareness of both our individual and collective realities, these in-between spaces become places of rich alchemical potential, and we begin to nurture a capacity to be present with the unknown, the not yet manifest, the fertile ground of all that's possible. And as our psyche learns to breathe into these portals of transformation, our abilities to welcome in the new, the never before imagined, begin to grow. From that, new forms, energies, and worlds can emerge because of our willingness to hold space for something that can only come to life in the quiet stillness between the known and unknown, between the manifest and the not yet manifest.

We're practicing that collectively as the old world dissolves and a new world rises.

Everything in our Universe is a sharing of energy; we're broadcasting our energies out into the world in every moment. What frequency are you radiating? What vibration are you magnetizing through what you're thinking and feeling? If it feels good, I'd love to invite you to look up toward the sky, take a deep breath, and offer a thank you to the Sun, the Moon, and the stars, hugging yourself and knowing that this miracle of now could not exist without your presence. As you breathe here, you could explore allowing your body to fully surrender into whatever support is beneath you or around you, attuning to the beauty of this moment, knowing that right now, through the gift of your presence, love itself is evolving.

Soul Nourishment

Connecting with the Moon and Sun is a powerful way to balance our inner lunar and solar energies or our feminine and masculine polarities. Two of my favorite ways to do this are to breathe intentionally with the sun at the beginning and end of each day. Even when it's cloudy or rainy, I turn my gaze in the direction of the sunrise and silently welcome the connection of my heart with the heart of the central sun. I rest here for as long as I'm able, breathing the new light into my cells and feeling it nourishing my own inner light. If I ever need a reset during the day, I again turn my gaze towards the sun and welcome the powerful solar light to cleanse and clear anything that needs releasing, while at the same time refreshing and restoring my own light. I do the same thing at sunset, giving thanks for the day and releasing anything ready to be surrendered.

I love connecting to the moon at any time during her phases, though when she's at or nearing fullness, I especially love the ritual of charging crystals, water, or other sacred creations in her brightness. If I'm able, I make a point to moonbathe, allowing the light to wash over my bare skin and nourish me with its sweet soma. Additionally, the moon offers a beautiful and safe space to share one's heart. Next time you're in her peaceful glow, explore sharing any concerns or prayers you have with her lunar grace, taking space to breathe with her light after you do, and then journaling about any guidance or wisdom you might receive from the communion.

CHAPTER 8: WATER

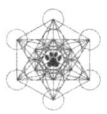

*"Your heart is the size of an ocean.
Go find yourself in its hidden depths."*
~Rumi

One of my favorite ways to experience life is swimming with Rumi under the endless blue skies of summer. The pine branches along the edge of Iris, our sacred forest lake, reflect the light sparkling on the water's surface as her little otter head swims by, intensely focused on finding a frog on the far shore. I can feel her joy and happiness through the water and sense her delight in my adoration as I cheer her on and swoon when we happen to brush against each other underwater during her determined pilgrimages from one shore to the other.

Equally charming is her signature wiggle and flip when I say, "Want to go to Iris?" as she instantly bursts into a huge grin while leaping in a little twirl of joy toward the door. This wasn't always the case. In her first year of healing, I tried introducing her to swimming as a possible way for her to get healthy movement during the many months she had severely limited mobility. She adamantly resisted swimming lessons at a friend's pool and showed no interest in Iris until one blessed day when her beloved auntie taught her the joy of chasing after sticks in the water. On that late spring day, she fell in love with swimming and hasn't looked back. Now, she'll spend hours on summer afternoons paddling serenely around Iris, pausing to inspect for frogs and delightedly exploring the water's edge for various discoveries. Often, she'll take herself for a swim, giving me a joyful glance of gratitude over her shoulder as she trots up the wooded path toward her little pocket of paradise. Some days, she'll be gone most of the afternoon, only to come barreling back down the hill, soaking wet and delightfully exhausted, ready to be toweled off and served her dinner, and then flopping down for a nap on the Sun-warmed river rock in front of the cabin, a smile of deep contentment stretched across her sleeping face.

Swimming with Rumi has been a profound teaching experience around the phenomenal power of water to transmit energies and as a medium for enlivening our awareness of the divinity within and all around.

In water, especially natural bodies of water that are in a pure state, frequencies can be elevated, even amplified, in ways that affect our existence through our perception of the information and vibration being translated.

I've had incredible experiences witnessing the profoundly healing power of water, and they've opened me to new ways of interacting with the water around me and within me, inspiring me to be even more conscious of how offering love and affirmation to the waters of life amplifies its potent healing energies for all of creation.

One such experience happened a few weeks ago. It had been a long day in town, and I came home to Rumi's sweet joy and enthusiasm at the suggestion of a late afternoon swim. I was floating on the calm surface of Iris and watching the clear blue sky and soft clouds above, my ears below the surface, immersed in the supreme quiet of the water, when all of a sudden, I heard the raucous sound of Rumi canon-balling into the water, her body and legs creating a cacophony of delight and activity, her paws peddling vigorously as she plowed past me after a potential frog sighting. The sounds reverberating through the water were amplified, as were the energies of her happiness and pure presence. I felt them reaching my ears and elevating my already awed state to one of pure rapture, the ripples of the water created by her paddling paws washing over my body like the caress of joy itself. The water translated her movement so I could both hear and feel her three-leggedness in the unique rhythm conveyed by the underwater sonics and the way the waves were washing against me. My heart melted in gratitude, remembering that she had once been afraid of the very water that had now become such a source of joy for her, as well as a space of healing. Often when she has played too hard and strained her leg, the best remedy is a swim in Iris. It seems to set something back into alignment, and I also sense that the healing energy of being in the water is in and of itself a tonic. Whether it's a natural body of water or a bathtub, shower or dancing in the rain, water carries potent healing energies that can elevate our consciousness, purify our minds, and bless us in profound ways, especially when we open ourselves to co-creation with the living consciousness that this sacred element holds through directing our intentions.

Another personal experience of the power of water happened when I was living in Hawai'i. One of my fondest memories from that time is of swimming with the wild dolphins at the black sand beach near my home. I would get up when the Sun was just beginning to rise and head down to the ocean in the early morning quiet to savor the new light of the dawning day in sacred solitude. My practice was to swim to distant lava rocks far out in the rich blue of the clear water, feeling the purification from being in water so deep and being so far away from other humans or land. Early on in the days of my morning swims, I became friends with the pod of wild dolphins who frequently visited that particular cove, and on days when I spied their happy fins bobbing along the surface, I would joyfully swim out to meet them, letting my body soften and my heart open as I neared them, offering tones of love under the water as I came closer.

One of their favorite ways to interact with me was to share the leaf they often played with, pushing it through the water or placing it on my body as I swam by. I would receive the leaf, usually a piece of one of the koa trees near the water's edge, and I would offer it back, all while we were swimming together in a wild dance of spirals and twists. Sometimes, they would swim around me in such passionate joy that the energy would move me bodily; I felt like a blessed rag doll being tossed around in the current of bliss created by their graceful arcs and dips. As it continued and intensified, I would feel myself going into an almost trance-like state, aware of both the water moving me about and the collaboration of play and love between us. I kept a shred of one of those leaves on my altar for many years, a reminder of those sacred communions of joy facilitated by the holy waters of Mama Ocean, holding us all in her healing arms. When I would later swim back to the beach, exhilarated and invigorated, I almost always felt reborn, aware that my internal waters had been elevated by the dolphins' frequency and the water's energy. It was as if our shared appreciation for the ocean and each other had created an alchemical reaction that had upgraded my whole system, leaving me with a sense of newness, of rebirth, that I knew was connected to the vibrational communication of the water itself.

Research worldwide has shown that human consciousness and environmental coherence can profoundly affect the molecular state of water, either enhancing its health-giving properties or reducing them. Veda Austin, Randy Hatton, and Masuro Emoto have shared fascinating evidence illustrating the power of thoughts, intentions, and environmental influences to affect the physical structure of water, thus demonstrating the power we have to uplift the well-being of all life on Earth as so much of the network of our earthly reality is made of water. The surface of the Earth is over seventy percent water, in addition to the vast reservoirs of water deep beneath the planet's surface, and humans are also over seventy percent water.

Because water has a divine, responsive intelligence, and since we're primarily made of water, what we think and say affects every cell in our bodies.

Water holds the light in our bodies, and when it's infused with love, it can hold even more light. If it feels good, try wrapping your arms around yourself and radiating love and appreciation to every cell of your being. You could explore doing this throughout the day, falling asleep in your own arms of love, waking up there in gratitude, and watching your whole world transform. You'll become so filled with light that you'll become the Homo Luminous being you're here to be, affecting those around you in the most beautiful ways. Infusing our internal watery landscapes with love raises our consciousness, and when we do this, we raise our personal and collective coherence.

We raise our coherence when we access emotions like joy, peace, compassion, and gratitude as our hearts and brains come into greater resonance, making the antennae of our bodies more finely tuned to attract similar frequencies in the external world. When we come into coherence, we access vibrational energy channels we couldn't before, elevating our toroidal fields—the electromagnetic fields that make up our auras—and the frequency of the world around us. We can positively affect the global consciousness by focusing our energies in ways that nurture this sense of coherence rather than focusing on the chaos, directing our planetary evolution toward a path of harmony. The HeartMath Institute has found that the heart's electrical field is about sixty times greater than the brain's electrical activity. This means that the heart conveys much more information to the brain than vice-versa, which debunks the idea that the brain is the predominant influencer in the body. When we're in a coherent state like gratitude or love, we enhance harmony in our fields. Coherence is when the heart, mind, and emotions are in energetic alignment and cooperation, and it builds physiological resilience, which equips us to handle the ebbs and flows of life better.

As we're all connected through water, it's one of the primary elements helping to raise our collective coherence and lead us into the new age. Our molecular structure is changing, and when we infuse the living waters we bring into our bodies and the waters of the world with loving intentions while also making environmentally sustainable choices, the healthier we and our planet become. We're electromagnetic beings; the more coherent we are, the stronger our electrical charge. As we purify our internal waters through our intentions and the blessings we offer to our water, we're supporting purifying the waters of the Earth that we all share. We're also liquid crystalline beings, and the water in the molecules of the breath we're breathing out into the world can uplift and enliven the water in the air being breathed in by all other beings.

The consciousness of the water in the air around you is being shaped by the consciousness you're breathing into it.

As you inhale deeply and receive the nourishment of this next breath, allow the vast peace in the center of your heart to infuse the molecules of water you're offering to the world around you. In this and every moment, we're shaping the flow of reality with the power of our hearts and infusing the living waters of existence with the light of our own loving awareness.

When we connect with the nature of water, we're connecting with ancient and future wisdom. Water invites us to dive into our depths, the mystery beneath the surface, and the fertility of the unseen and unknown within. Water is life, and its unplumbed depths remind us of the new life teeming within our vessels, waiting for the right time to emerge and bring new direction and illumination to our personal and collective journeys. The liquid magma below the planet's surface births new earth; the lava that flows from this dark womb creates ground for new life to grow. This aliveness hidden within our planetary body is the same mysterious life force pulsing within each of us.

The same divine intelligence that creates miracles in the Universe is alive in every cell of our beings, simply waiting for the right conditions to flow forth in newly imagined manifestations of divinity in form.

Water invites us to engage with this inner life force, to acknowledge and commune with this incredible power in order to welcome it more consciously into our lives in the interest of bringing forth new potentials for ourselves and our world. It welcomes us into the rich silence and stillness within our depths, and in this, to surrender the limitations of the known world to make space for what's yet to emerge, softening into the new and all possible as a radical act of faith and courage.

Almost fifty percent of water on Earth is up to 4.5 billion years old, and it came from outer space, from asteroids and stars, and the ice that's held within interstellar dust. Because of water's ancient and cosmic origins, it offers a divine intelligence and sacred healing energy to our evolving consciousness. It invites us to explore our own fluidity and open ourselves to the possibility of transformation contained within every breath. When we truly embrace this potential for change, we open ourselves even more deeply to the blessings of our imaginations and our creative powers, allowing us to surrender to the divine flow of grace that water offers to our earthly existence. All of the water on our forest homestead comes from the rain we catch off the roof, and even after years of living this way, I'm still in awe every day of the miracle of clean, healthy water. Water is life; if you're blessed to have clean water for drinking and bathing, give thanks and make the choices to support this as a reality for all beings. Feel the gratitude for clean water for all flowing in every cell of your body and uplifting the vibration of your energy field. The consciousness of the water in each of your molecules responds to your appreciation. When breathed out, it uplifts the energies around you, bringing us all into greater coherence and alignment in this very moment.

Water reflects to us the power of our thoughts and intentions and rewards us with enhanced well-being and cellular rejuvenation.

We're in a place of taking radical responsibility for our world, as every word and action we offer affects everything else.

I invite you to let go of ever calling a human or more-than-human being "bad," as everyone is doing the best they can with the resources they have. Everything we do, say, and think matters. As we break our addiction to a consciousness of separation and judgment, we're interrupting an outworn pattern. We're reshaping the morphogenetic fields we're passing along to future generations and encoding them with habits of harmony and cooperation. Because water connects and nourishes all of life on Earth, every blessing we offer to it is a blessing for all. I give thanks to the raindrops as they fall, to my water before drinking or bathing, to the clouds in the sky above me, to the humidity in the summer air, and to the sacred waters in the bodies of those I hug. Every moment offers an opportunity to receive the grace of the sacred waters sustaining us and to offer praise to the waters within and around us, uplifting all of life through the power of our loving intentions.

Soul Nourishment

Offering blessings to our inner and outer waters is a beautiful way to explore the power of love to shift the energies within and around us. The consciousness of water responds to any loving intentions we offer, and as there is water in every living thing, in the molecules of air we breathe, and in the core of the earth herself, our power to positively influence reality is limitless in scope. You can explore this by simply giving yourself a hug and offering a silent wave of I love you's, breathing slowly and noticing how you feel as your cells receive this loving kindness. Next, you can try extending this to the more than human kindred around you, inviting yourself to tune into the flow of grace moving between your heart and those receiving your love. Then, explore sending it out the furthest reaches of the Universe, feeling it moving in a wave of light, blessing all who encounter its power. When you're taking a bath or shower or near a natural body of water, explore offering this blessing of I love you's and pause to witness any energetic shifts you notice as the water receives this offering of your heart. If you have a worry or concern, imagine offering it to the water, inviting it to be embraced and transformed by this healing force. Giving thanks to the water for its powers of purification, conclude by offering an affirmation of love to your own inner waters as you move forward with renewed peace.

CHAPTER 9: EMBODIMENT

"Your heart knows the way. Run in that direction."
~Rumi

It was late spring, and I had ventured out barefoot early one morning to the open space beside the cabin. The golden rays of the dawning sunlight streamed through the treetops as baby birdsong floated through the air in sweet brushstrokes of joy. I was edging carefully along the mini-wetlands that formed every spring, my eyes out for the tiny baby turtles I had seen just days before, their soft round shells no bigger than a walnut. My eyes were drawn to a gentle rustle by my feet as I looked down to see a mature painted lady turtle climbing steadily along the sloping landscape. I leaned down to marvel at her gorgeous coloring, fiery orange and deep auburn weaving a sacred geometry of aliveness across her shell when an amazed smile spread across my face as I witnessed that she was three-legged! Not only that, but she was also missing the same leg as Rumi, her back right, and she was moving with a power and sureness that nearly brought me to my knees in awe. In reverence, I kneeled down to see if she needed any help. However, closer inspection revealed that the long-ago injury had healed up perfectly, leaving her fully mobile and capable as she lumbered along the forest floor with a slightly wobbly but confident gait. I hadn't ever even imagined a three-legged turtle, and of all the miles of forest for her to choose to call home, she had ended up here, right outside our door, just steps from Basil's three-legged bones and right under the nose of Rumi's tri-pawed majesty. How had this precious being lost its leg, and how had it managed to survive and thrive in this altered state? I spent the rest of the season in deepening wonder, quietly visiting her nest of leaves and offering my silent praise for her strength and grace as I beheld the magnificence of her presence. Rumi joined me, often standing by in silent camaraderie with this kindred turtle soul, with whom she shared both her forest home and her unique embodiment journey.

In some ways, we all share a unique embodiment journey, and embracing this can help us become open to a more harmonious way of being alive together as we simultaneously hold awareness of our diversity in our unity. The aliveness we share unites us across any categorical lines of separation; we're all perfect, whole, and complete exactly as we are, and nothing is missing, broken, or wrong with any of us.

We're all worthy of love, kindness, and care, and a world built on this foundation of justice is the only one in which all can truly thrive.

As we come into wholeness within ourselves by honoring all of the pieces and parts that make us uniquely who we are, we can mirror this safety and acceptance to the world around us. Cultural conditioning has resulted in an illusion of "normalcy" and standards of beauty and worth that are unrealistic and harmful. The awe-inspiring three-legged turtles and the spectacular trees split down the middle by lightning remind us of the perfection inherent in each of us in every moment, exactly as it is and exactly as we are. We can practice welcoming our whole selves home with loving appreciation, especially the parts we have deemed broken or unworthy, and back into the Eden we knew deep in our bones before separation clouded our vision. This is the key to releasing resistance to the wild blessing that is our one precious life and to fully honoring the experience of being alive as it comes. This allows us to ride the waves that naturally arise rather than getting pulled under by them. When we stop waiting for life to show up in a certain way or trying to force ourselves to conform to an expectation of worth, we experience life as it is and tap into the wisdom that naturally flows from this state of loving awareness for ourselves and all others.

The divine source that birthed the Universe, the energy that's unknowable, and also the one thing we know most truly, is who we all are. This remembrance of what we're actually embodying is the gateway to self-actualization and coming into harmony with our divinity and humanity, our form and formlessness in union. We are not our personalities or stories; we are the living light that is so much closer. If it feels good, I'd love to invite you to pause and breathe into what is closer than any thoughts or narratives you've had about yourself and to feel the profound simplicity and beauty available in that awareness. If, for one minute a day, we could stop to breathe into the closeness of our true selves and practice witnessing the true self in others that is so much more real than our opinions or judgments, a new world would emerge. When I breathe into this as I'm present with a tree, or Rumi, or the scent of lilac, I feel the space between my divinity and humanity dissolving, and I witness how the more-than-human realm is ever-reflecting this loving reality that many humans tend to forget. These wise teachers are patiently and gently inviting us into remembrance, into accepting our individuality and wholeness in every moment if we so choose. The natural world is always mirroring this truth to us; from the butterflies with tattered wings soaring all summer long from zinnia to sunflower with dazzling confidence, to the three-legged turtles who awe us with their strength and beauty, it's inviting us to embrace the diversity of energies within ourselves and each other by practicing compassion for our unique soul journeys in the wild adventure of life.

Universe means "one song," and it's the variety of notes and the spaces between the notes that create the integrity of the song. As the dwarf planet Quaoror reflects, we are being sung and danced into a new way of being, and all of us are needed to bring this new world into existence. How can we fine-tune our individual notes to come into harmony with the larger grace being sung by the greater consciousness of reality? In this moment, can I receive a deep breath of peace and soften my heart, offering an exhalation of loving kindness to the world around me, knowing that doing so will shift the vibration of my molecules in such a way that will be uplifting to myself and all others? I can, I am, and I will, again and again, because I know that every time I do, that flame of faith nestled deep in the womb of my soul is expanding, growing stronger, and becoming a beacon for those calling for support, lighting the way home to the loving arms awaiting us all.

In the midst of the chaos of the old world dissolving, we can commit to a new, better version of life, and we can steadfastly breathe allegiance into this emergent reality.

We can be creative warriors devoted to a path of care that honors the sacred flame of divinity in all. As we do so, we witness our individual flames growing larger, uniting with the flames of others who are breathing life into this shared vision, until we're all gathered at the divine hearth of our collective light, beholding the rising of the phoenix from the ashes of the old in a new paradigm of peace.

While we may not embody this state of oneness and harmony in every moment, being intentional about presence can help us navigate the places of contrast that naturally arise along the earthly journey. Sometimes, a few deep breaths, or a conscious invitation for assistance from the divine, or the engagement of any other mindfulness tools I might choose, support me in moving through the inevitable ebbs and flows of life with much greater ease.

Like healing in the physical body, when we can let go of contraction and tension, healing occurs much more easefully.

The tissues are better able to receive the *pranic*, or life force, nourishment that naturally flows when we're relaxed, and we can then recover more fully and swiftly than when in a state of resistance or tightness.

I experienced a profound opening to the power our bodies possess as instruments of healing and atlases of our soul's journey when I attended my first yoga class at age twenty. I was living in France at the time, with only one friend, and working in a cafe where I was struggling to navigate each day with rudimentary French and a very harsh boss. I was getting by, though I sensed something simmering just below the surface of my emotional awareness. When I walked into that first yoga class, a warm, welcoming French woman greeted me kindly and guided me to a sunny spot in front of the big windows facing the tree-lined boulevard of the tiny studio. Toward the middle of the class, she led us gently into *matsyasana*, or fish pose. As my heart and neck opened wide in the gentle inversion, I felt a wave of deep emotion begin to course through me, a waterfall of tears cascading from my eyes, and all I could do was surrender, the tears flowing freely as I felt lifetimes of suppressed sadness being freed from my body. I spent the remainder of the class mostly in child's pose, my head tucked into the safety of my own energy, letting the tears flow and feeling the tender softening that had longed to be felt for years. The kind instructor gave me the sweetest hug, murmuring soothing words of affirmation in French when the class ended. I felt a sense of kinship and being known, which touched my heart with a deep love that carried me as I cried for a week straight, finally allowing years of repressed feelings to be felt and released. At the end of the week, I felt like a new person. A clarity and inner strength that I had never known before was pulsing in my veins, and the fear that had been released had created space for new light to fill my being. A few weeks later, I sat and watched the Sun rise over the distant Alps, feeling receptive to this dawning energy in a way I had never thought possible.

When we let go of what no longer serves us, we create space for new light to nourish and elevate us into higher dimensions of embodiment.

These dimensions align us with the love that guides us home to ourselves and toward our shared destiny of cooperative compassion.

The new light we create space for transforms our human architecture. As it streams onto our planet and activates dormant DNA, we embody more of our soul selves, which have an unlimited capacity to transform and adapt to new ways of existing and interrelating. As we evolve our ability to express as fractals of Source consciousness in an expanding Universe, our capacity to focus on the positive evolution of humanity becomes one of our greatest gifts and resources. We influence each other by reflecting new ways of being and understanding the purpose and potential of our shared journey. We see what we look for and can attune our vision to notice miracles rather than danger. We can invite our brains to witness moments of beauty and pause to give thanks.

A Buddhist practice called "gladdening the heart" teaches that when we bring thoughts centered in love and appreciation into our hearts, that energy will increase in our awareness, and we'll attract more of the experiences that lead to those feelings. The Law of Attraction teaches that manifestation kicks in when we can focus on something for at least seventeen seconds. When we bring the two together in a practice of intending to notice and lingering in appreciation for the many positive occurrences around us, more of that energy will grow on the planet. The natural realm is constantly offering us opportunities for appreciation by showing us visions of the vast beauty and exquisite harmony possible for our world, and we can begin embodying more of these qualities ourselves as we tune our awareness to focus on these gifts of grace.

Embodiment is a portal into our current evolutionary leap, and the more-than-human realm has great wisdom for this area of our transformation as a species. Our material form is a medium for expressing our divinity; as it's malleable, we can support our evolution as a species to become a more compassionate version of ourselves through conscious collaboration with the natural world. We're easily influenced, and as sovereign beings, we essentially have free will over where we focus our attention, and where we direct attention is what gets fed in the gardens of our growth.

As I write, I look out on a sea of green—oak, maple, and redbud—fresh life surrounding me in all directions. The sunlight sparkles on their leaves in quiet luminescence, while the breeze creates a soft orchestra of magic in the green-golden light as it dances through. I look up intermittently to breathe in this wild and sacred beauty and offer a smile of gratitude and a deep exhale of blessing for all the trees; every time I do so, my heart opens even wider. We can begin inviting ourselves to breathe in conscious connection with the trees, to offer the gift of our CO_2 with intention, and to receive the gift of their oxygen-filled expressions with appreciation. The molecules entering our lungs are then charged with the prana, life force energy, of this holy exchange, while the world around us elevates through the love we're breathing out. This is just an example of one small step we might take, a one-degree shift in conscious presence and collaboration that we can explore, that can beneficially impact the Earth and our embodiment in astounding ways.

Every time, I'm in awe of the way I sense the green world responding to this offering of love; the presence of the divine is palpable, the softening of my heart is magical, and the evolution of my awareness is profound. Sometimes, I like to think of someone I know or someone I'll never know and intentionally breathe out the love I'm feeling, knowing that somehow, somewhere, they'll feel it, and it will change their world for the better.

An admirable aspiration for life is that each moment you encounter is enhanced simply by coming into contact with your loving awareness.

The trees model this, as do the flowers, the birds, our sacred companion animals, and the Sun and Moon, as they mirror our shared sacredness in their very existence.

Chapter 9: Embodiment

The increased solar activity is bringing new light to our planet, prompting significant changes. Our bodies are transitioning into a crystalline state, allowing us to hold more light, which in turn is driving the evolution of our DNA. After lifetimes of existing in a carbon-based form, our bodies are alchemizing the new photonic light in ways that shift our internal structures into more crystalline forms, allowing us to literally hold more light to enlighten. Our senses serve as a gateway to this new potential for embodiment, acting as a medium for interconnection and subtle transformation. By intending to develop a specific sense, such as sight, we can both shape our personal embodiment and influence the world around us. Our more-than-human allies guide us in this realm, inviting us into presence as a means of communion with the divine, allowing us to recognize the divinity in all things. We can connect with all of creation through sensorial communion, such as touch or sound—laying our hands on trees or harmonizing with birds.

Our intention to consciously co-create opens a doorway for emergent possibilities that shape us in new and transformative ways.

I witnessed the transformative power of sensorial intimacy during an extraordinary exchange between Tina, a shaman grandmother guinea pig, and Rumi, one early spring afternoon. We were visiting a friend, a devoted guinea pig mama, and she had her beloved piggies out in the yard to savor the fresh air and light. Rumi has an incredibly strong prey drive and is a phenomenal hunter, so I had her on a leash as we approached the pigs. Rumi was straining at the leash, her muscles engaged, and her eyes focused intently on pouncing on the pigs. I held her tightly and encouraged her to relax. As we neared the area where the pigs were grazing, Tina, the elder of the bunch, calmly turned toward us, still peacefully chewing her clover leaves, and slowly reached her nose up toward Rumi. I watched in awe as Rumi looked into Tina's eyes with wild wonder, incredulous that this tiny creature was showing no fear whatsoever and was extending a warm welcome to her despite Rumi's obvious predatory energy. After several moments of observing Rumi's deep concentration in awed silence as she struggled to make sense of what was happening, I saw her suddenly relax. Her whole body exhaled in complete peace as she lay down beside the enclosed area, gently reaching her nose out to softly touch Tina's, the sunlight sparkling like stars in their eyes as they breathed together, nose to nose, in reverent presence. From that moment on, Rumi lay adoringly beside the pigs, watching with devotion as they savored the afternoon. Tina would occasionally come back over to quietly touch her nose up to meet Rumi's in the holiest of blessings. In that initial exchange, I witnessed Rumi completely rewrite the narrative of her embodiment, choosing to release generations of programming in order to explore a brand-new way of being alive. I observed the power of love from Tina, who was a fraction of Rumi's size, to inspire an evolutionary leap toward harmony and cooperation that resulted in a depth of loving intimacy that may have seemed impossible just moments before. Tina embodied the wisdom and power we all possess to offer this frequency of loving kindness in ways that forever alter the world around us, inspiring a kinship of care for all of creation. As Shakespeare so eloquently wrote, "One touch of nature makes the whole world kin." Collaborating with the higher wisdom of the natural realm by exploring embodied intimacy can open new doorways of communion to exchange energy in innovative ways that support miraculous evolutionary shifts for all of life on Earth.

The dawning Symbiocene Era highlights the profound influence we have on our evolutionary path through the frequency we embody, shaped by our intention, attention, and mindfulness.

As we develop our sixth sense, the inner eye, we become more attuned to the life-enhancing energies offered by the natural world.

During this radical shift in our three-dimensional reality, it's essential to balance both inner and outer focus. Over-focusing on the external can cause us to overlook the deep inner evolution happening alongside the transformation of the outer world around us.

Directing our awareness to the *nous*, the eye of the heart, is a potent support on this transformational journey. Nous is the Greek word for mind, and the Mary Magdalene Gospels describe it as a portal to see through the vision of the soul, as it's a concept of the mind that includes the heart as an organ of spiritual perception necessary for clear seeing. Perceiving reality through the inner eye of the heart allows us to focus on the heart's vision of a harmonious world, and it invites us to live from a simplicity and innocence that's a soothing balm for a culture of over-stimulated nervous systems. *Merkaba,* an ancient Egyptian term meaning "soul light body" or "chariot of the soul," refers to the sacred fields of light that support us on our incarnational journeys. This chariot encompasses our physical and energetic bodies, inviting a deeper understanding of how our human and divine natures manifest in our lived experiences. Often depicted as a sacred geometric field surrounding the human body, the Merkaba envelops us in light as we navigate the earthly realm.

When we perceive ourselves as Hierogamic, *in a state of inner union with our humanity and divinity, we expand our awareness of our potential as souls of light.*

This perspective allows us to view incarnation as an opportunity for co-creative alchemy and awakening. *Hieros Gamos* signifies the realization of the body within the infinite light of divine consciousness, symbolizing the resurrection of the original divine essence in every living being.

We can help activate new parts of our light bodies and encourage the crystallization of our forms through a cornucopia of different practices; the key is to listen for what feels best for you. One of my favorite practices is to ask myself, "How can I love you better?" and simply witness what arises. This is a beautiful question to ask anyone, and it's a cornerstone of compassionate communication in all of my relationships, human and more-than-human. Another good inquiry for supporting the crystallization process is exploring what grounds you in your body. One of my favorite ways to ground myself is being barefoot on the earth, especially on moss. That's part of how I knew this forest was home for us, as there are carpets of moss all over the wooded hillsides. It feels like plugging into something so loving and reliable, and it helps me remember the mountain that I am and root into that grounded wisdom within.

Direct contact with the earth, trees, stones, or other natural elements is fabulously beneficial for the nervous system and our overall well-being. I aim for at least twenty minutes daily of skin-to-earth contact, usually by walking barefoot or working in the garden. However, any amount of time is wonderful and will boost antioxidants in the body and help clear toxins and stressful emotional debris. If you don't have access to that type of engagement, holding a stone or crystal, touching a house plant, or receiving direct sunlight or moonlight can be just as supportive and nourishing.

Direct natural light can greatly benefit our glandular system. Exposing the third eye, located at the pituitary gland, to early morning sunlight helps decalcify the pineal gland, often referred to as the seat of the soul. Situated deep in the center of the brain, directly behind the pituitary gland, the pineal gland contains light-sensitive cells that secrete melatonin and regulate our circadian rhythms. Many wisdom traditions view the pineal gland as a bridge between the physical and spiritual realms, and supporting this area of the body intentionally can lead to profound evolutionary shifts. Besides exposure to early morning sunlight and moonlight, other practices can help activate the pineal gland and facilitate consciousness expansion. These include drinking plenty of pure water, intentionally breathing through the third-eye area, focusing attention on it during meditation, and anointing it with sacred oils or plants. I love to put a single rose petal or leaf of lemon balm on my third eye and breathe for several minutes, allowing the grace of the natural realm to infuse my awareness with its wisdom.

Becoming more intentional about our evolutionary embodiment is sacred medicine for our transforming world.

The *kundalini*, divine life-force energy, is rising within the Earth and within our own bodies, and the more conscious we become of how to engage this pranic potential in collaboration with the intelligence of the natural realm, the more we can evolve.

It's a privilege to be embodied on this Earth, as these sacred forms of flesh and blood offer us the opportunity to savor and experience the magnificence of sensual incarnation and the beauty that comes with that. We're energy beings in human form, and the *chakra* system, an ancient map of the multidimensional energy body, is helpful in realizing the power in this embodiment more fully. Chakras are energy centers that reflect different qualities of our existence in our individual and collective journeys, and when we work to care for ourselves and each other from this holistic perspective of wholeness, we're unlimited in our healing potential. When we understand the energetic interconnection of all of life, we witness the power we have to affect positive change on a global scale. The indigenous wisdom of being in sacred collaboration with all of life is inviting us to become more aware of the power we hold in every breath, thought, and action to positively influence ourselves, and also the collective, in ways that will only be beneficial for those who follow in our footsteps. This sacred guidance from the natural realm is inspiring an embodiment of our greatness in ways we've only begun to envision.

When we view existence from this multidimensional, holistic perspective, we embrace death as an integral part of the creative spiral. Holding sacred space for sweet Basil during the months when he walked from his earthly existence into his world beyond form was one of the holiest experiences I've ever known. He showed me the exquisite beauty in the softening of the soul's grip on earthly life and the power in alchemizing essence into expansion.

When we view death as the blessed part of the embodiment journey that it is, we come into greater presence with love itself.

The natural world models this in the seasonal changes of autumn and winter, inviting us to feel the gift in this time of death and letting go as we create space for something new and unknown to show up. Letting go requires radical faith; instead of seeking security and safety from the known, we're invited to remember it within. As we do, we become a source of that inner peace in the world, radiating it out to all creation.

Welcoming death as part of the wholeness of our soul's journey allows us to expand into the fullness of who we are, inviting greater awareness of our sense of belonging in the sacred spiral of existence, which in turn helps us perceive our interbeingness with all of life. In this, we understand how who we choose to be in this life informs all of the life that will come after us and how it influences our soul's journey as we travel beyond this dimension when this lifetime is over. We're all evolving together, and as we expand our understanding of who we are on a soul level, we elevate our vibrational expressions, which uplifts the collective consciousness. Everything is vibration, and it's mingling and alchemizing all the time. Our capacity to hold a greater knowing of who we are as energetic beings who aren't limited by unhelpful binary systems or cultural constructs allows us to tap into our boundless potential. When we hold a more affirming and inclusive space for ourselves as individuals, we invite the spaciousness to explore our evolving potential as a collective.

This softening around constrictions of identity allows us to more fully embody our soul selves, supporting a more harmonious existence for all beings. Releasing the unhelpful gender binary from my awareness brought a profound sense of peace and presence into my life, as I felt a more expansive sense of belonging in the broader tapestry of life. When I first heard the term "nonbinary," I interpreted it as an invitation to embrace the true self I'd always known yet had never had language for, the one that's part wolf, moonlight, pine tree, rose quartz, and mountain. However, for most people, nonbinary often relates to how one identifies in terms of gender; as both my divine feminine and masculine have always felt powerfully alive in my sense of who I am, it was fantastic to embrace this enhanced spaciousness for self-expression that felt truer to my essence. I feel a natural ebb and flow of masculine and feminine energies in myself and the world around me that fluctuate depending on the season or my internal rhythms.

The fact that the collective conversation is now creating space for expressions of self beyond the binary system speaks to the greater consciousness expansion around what it even means to be human.

I'm my full self in my masculinity and femininity, my humanness and more-than-humanness, my uniqueness, and my intrinsic belonging to the greater whole. My true identity is loving awareness, witnessing the grace breathing through every molecule of existence.

What is as yet undeveloped in language that will allow us to expand even more deeply into a truer, more aligned appreciation of ourselves and each other? How we identify is how we understand our sense of belonging. When we recognize that we belong simply because we're here, we radiate this compassionate care to all of life on Earth, and in knowing that all belong to each other, we make choices that uplift the good of all of creation.

When we lean into our ability to hold space for the wholeness of who we are individually and collectively, quantum shifts occur in our reality because innate in this welcoming of our all-ness is the celebration of our spiritual selves. This embodiment of our divine nature brings radical transformation into our world, as spiritual presence is unbounded by the limitation of time, space, and what we think is possible. So, while we may not see the complete realization of a new paradigm of peace in this lifetime, we'll see tremendous progress toward its manifestation. When we open our awareness to the intelligence of the more-than-human realm, we remember that perceived "problems" are often gateways to miracles. As I write this, there are over eight billion humans on the planet, which many perceive as a problem. However, when we recognize that our thoughts and vibrations are creating our reality, we see the mass awakening that's possible when enough hearts and minds come together and focus on a just world. The divine integrity in bringing our individual intentions together in a shared vision of harmony is the doorway to the global shift that we've come here to birth.

We're so much more than we've been taught; we are divinity itself, the original face of Goddex, the light of the world. This truth is embedded in all the wisdom traditions, from Sanskrit mantras like *sat nam*, my name is truth, to the Hawaiian *Ha* breath that carries Source love.

Every molecule of our existence radiates divinity, and when we allow this divinity to infuse our awareness of who we are and who we're becoming, individually and collectively, anything is possible.

This is an invitation to a revolution, to embody the supreme grace and boundless power that we are when we embrace our belonging in the collective web of creation we're weaving together.

Soul Nourishment

Supporting our embodiment as we navigate the powerful ascension process we're in is integral to being able to most fully receive its blessings. Any grounding and heart-centering practices will be supportive, and some of my favorites are earthing, gladdening the heart, and nourishing the light body. Earthing is simply walking barefoot on the ground, allowing your feet to absorb Gaia's healing nutrients and grounding energies for as long as it feels good. You can also sit, stand still, or lie down; the idea is to have direct skin contact with the Earth and to consciously attune to the healing flow of love that happens in that communion. The Buddhist practice of gladdening the heart, focusing your attention in your heart center and bringing to your awareness someone you love who brings you a sense of peace and love, is another wonderful way to support your greatest well-being. You can focus here for a while and then direct that loving energy out to the world around you, and then back to your own heart in a wave of appreciation. Concluding by asking, "How can I love you better?" offers a beautiful invitation to relax any limitations you might have had around who you are or who you might be becoming, and it's a wonderful way to offer nourishment to the ongoing evolutionary adventure that your body is offering to you in every moment.

CHAPTER 10: AMBROSIA

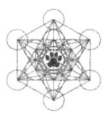

"Be with those who help your being."
~Rumi

It was late evening, and we had just watched the Sun sink slowly into the green horizon. Rumi had already gotten ready for bed, her teeth brushed, PJs on, and bedtime snacks consumed; however, evening gardening was too tempting for me to resist, so she sleepily padded along behind as I made my way up the path. There's something so sweet about gardening at sunset as the forest quiets all around and the plants begin their inward turn for the night. Sometimes, I wonder if plants dream; I like to think that they do, their petals curling into soft smiles as they dream of quenching rains and warm sunlight nourishing their growing bodies.

After some idle weeding and general puttering, I noticed the carrot tops waving gently in the breeze. Finally, they seemed tall enough to have a potential orange root growing under the soil surface. This was a prized patch of carrots, mostly because I'd only planted a few that season, and they're one of Rumi's and my favorite and oft-savored vegetables. With slightly held breath, I gently eased one from the soil, and as it emerged, my heart opened wide with wonder. She was the most gorgeous carrot I had ever beheld. Her texture was perfect, firm, and inviting, and her soft, earthy scent was almost intoxicating. For a quiet moment, I reveled in her simple beauty before I heard, "Give it to Rumi." Of course, this prized creation was destined for the mouth of my babe, who was curled sweetly in a little patch of clover, snoozing peacefully with a slight smile on her lips. I went over to gently rouse her, and she sleepily parted her jaws with expectant appreciation. What followed stretched the smile in my heart even wider as she purposefully munched it down, the sounds of her happy crunching mingling with her slight air of entitlement as she knew she would be the recipient of this earthly treasure. The sound of her eating always brings a smile to my soul, but this moment expanded that joy exponentially as I could hear the freshness of the carrot bursting with each bite, the prana flowing directly into her body, and her joy in the deliciousness of our shared appreciation of the moment. A wave of delight swept through the space with the gorgeous dusky night beginning to embrace the forest in her welcoming arms, the blessed sound of Rumi savoring sustenance from the Earth, and me, loving it all and reveling in the beauty of such sweet alchemy. This was one of many moments that felt like grace to me; my deep gratitude for the nourishment being offered by this planet married with my reverence for the everyday miracles all around us (like carrots) and beholding the ones we love receiving these gifts.

How we nourish ourselves and each other is a key component of birthing a just world for all beings, and bringing greater intentionality and appreciation to what we support with our food choices is integral to creating this justice on our planet. Bringing even small practices of connection and gratitude to what we put in our bodies can create a radical shift in our choices, as it invites us into an even greater presence with how we feed ourselves and each other. Tuning into what the season is offering is a good step toward bringing greater awareness to our consumption habits, and even living in an urban area, one can explore the wild edibles that might be growing in different seasons. In my earlier years of city living, I grew sprouts and herbs on my windowsill. I went to our local park to harvest wild dandelions, violets, red clover, berries, garlic mustard, and chickweed. It gave me an opportunity to connect more intimately with how and what I was eating. Even in major urban areas, I've found edible plants and medicine growing in abandoned lots, through sidewalk cracks, and along the perimeters of city parks. However, before foraging there, I always ensured that the areas were free from pesticides and other harmful chemicals. And as always, I thanked the wild world for its humbling and breathtaking generosity.

Living in the forest and having space for gardening has only deepened my awareness of how vital it is to shift our global relationship with food and nourishment toward justice and sustainability. Creating space to

Chapter 10: Ambrosia

appreciate the food growing around us and savor this gift of sustenance has deepened my awe for the love the earth offers. Attuning to the natural cycles by engaging with these plants has nurtured a profound understanding of the collaborative potential available through more conscious food choices.

One of our favorite summer routines is to hike up the ridge to watch the sunrise, where Rumi goes straight to the blackberry bushes, her nose sniffing carefully as she attempts to suss out the ripe ones. There are few things more endearing than watching her pick berries off the bush with her mouth, her sweet teeth delicately plucking them from the stems, hoping for a ripe one. Mostly, I do the picking, as she's realized that my longer arms and legs allow me to land the most prime specimens, and she knows I always offer her the best ones. We stand side by side, her nose tucked into the bushes by my knees while I alternate between picking and reaching down to place them in her happy, waiting mouth. Although they're the most delicious berries I've ever tasted, the joy I feel from the entire experience is the most nourishing part. Heading home, feeling the freshness of the berries revitalizing my body and Rumi's, I always feel a dimension of gratitude that transcends words. To live in a world where we can enjoy the nourishment and pleasure of a wild blackberry and share it with someone we love is a holy miracle and a reflection of the beauty of nature itself.

The marker that blackberry season is around the corner happens when the garlic is ready to harvest. The tall green fronds begin to list as the days lengthen and the Sun grows stronger. This year, it was early June when I heard the garlic calling to me, her outer leaves beginning to dry out and change color as a demonstration of her ripeness. It was already evening, but rain was predicted to come at night, so I knew it was time to dig the bulbs from the ground and begin their curing process. I gathered a sheet to carry the harvest and headed up to the garden, Rumi falling sleepily behind as the Sun slowly began to set. About a third of the way through, with an impressive mini-mountain of garlic beginning to form, she scratched out a little bed in the leaves and soil, circling neatly into it to continue monitoring my progress. As I neared the halfway point, she looked up at me, yawning, and slowly went down to the front porch, where she could participate from the comfort of her bed. As the last whispers of daylight wafted through the forest, I gathered the harvest in the wagon, my fingers blessed with the scent of fresh garlic and rich earth, and made my way down to the cabin.

Soon after garlic-harvesting time, when the honeybees are floating gracefully through the air rapturously laden with bright orange pollen, another garden wonder emerges as the tomatoes ripen. We'd been watching the first one slowly plumpening on the vine, her ruby roundness growing fuller each day. Late one early July afternoon, when I went to pick vegetables for dinner, I knew it was time. Her heavy red fruit felt like home in my hand, and I couldn't even make it the few steps back to the sanctuary before biting into her perfect, warm flesh, rich tomato deliciousness saturating my taste buds and filling my mouth with bliss. I don't even consider myself a tomato lover. However, there's nothing that compares to harvesting and savoring the first tomato of summer, the particular and unique combination of flavor and texture that only comes around when the days are long and the air is warm.

When tomato season comes to a close, it feels like the signal of a bigger shift, one in which my internal rhythm begins turning toward fall as the garden begins to conclude the robustness of its summer abundance. This intimacy with the seasonal shifts is one of the many things I love about gardening; it brings me into greater alignment with the natural world and gives me even deeper reverence for the earthly nourishment that blesses our lives so generously. The longer I grow my own food, the deeper my gratitude becomes for the blessing of nurturing something from seed to harvest, singing and tending to its development for months, and then gratefully receiving its healing prana when its cycle is complete. The feeling when I bite into a freshly picked spinach leaf and feel it revitalizing my cells is one of humble awe; I bow to the plants, the Sun, the rain, and all of the millions of energies that bring this sacred sustenance to our lives.

Caring for Rumi has brought me an even deeper appreciation for the healing power of fresh, healthy food and the gift of sharing that with those we love. When the Humane Society took her in, she was practically emaciated, and her bones were visible through her skin. Five years later,

Chapter 10: Ambrosia

her attitude toward food still reflects a rough beginning around nourishment, and I feel tremendous gratitude whenever I place a meal in front of her. She loves all food and savors everything with great gusto, which is one of the many reasons I love making her food myself. She thinks she has one of the best jobs on the planet because twice a month, she gets to clean the pots from the creation of her ambrosia. She always knows when it's Ambrosia Day, which, in her opinion, is one of the two best days of the month. On those days, we get out the crockpot and make her food for the next two weeks. It's a multi-hour event involving a variety of pans and containers that require her astute cleaning abilities.

The preparations begin early in the day when I get the pot out and start simmering the foundational ingredients. The creation of the bounty involves many different stages and phases, and she carefully monitors my work, usually sitting right at my feet and watching every chop and cut with a keen eye. If something happens to distract me from the current task at hand, like a phone call coming in or an irresistible beckoning to tend to something outside, she lets me know with clarity that my variance from the job is not only unacceptable but requires a firm reprimand and clear direction to get back to work immediately. I call her food "ambrosia, food of the goddesses," because she is indeed holy, and her food is definitely fit for any divine canine. I switched from feeding her packaged dog food the first year she came into my life at the urging of her vet, and I haven't looked back since. It may take a little more time, but it's well worth it, and her vitality and wellness prove that it's benefiting her tremendously. Something about choosing to make the effort to cook for her and witnessing how I can infuse her food with love shifted me into an even deeper intimacy with her and brought me an even greater appreciation for the power of conscious food choices in creating a world of right relationship with all of creation.

Not only is what we feed ourselves important in how it drastically influences our well-being and development in mind, body, and spirit, but it also plays a crucial role in restructuring a world built on a foundation of domination and exploitation. Coming into conscious relationship with our world entails shifting our personal choices so that resources can be more justly distributed, thus ensuring that all beings are well-nourished.

Even though this planet has more than enough resources to feed everyone, so many are undernourished.

A massive shift is already underway as more humans wake up to the power we possess in choosing to live simply so that others may simply live.

For many, this means eating a primarily plant-based, local, regeneratively grown diet if possible. It means if you're eating animal products and can, choose ones that are raised humanely and regeneratively so that the waterways and soil are being tended to responsibly. It might mean eating out less so that you have more resources available to support local organic farmers, and it means supporting initiatives that are helping to feed those in need and restoring lands that have been degraded due to large-scale agriculture. There are so many ways we can become more caring and responsible consumers; having the intention to live more simply and taking daily actions to support this intention is an excellent first step. Every choice we make to live more gently on the planet matters, and right now, we can make choices around what we consume that will benefit the next seven generations and beyond. It's not too late, and it's possible; it all matters. Even a single shift in purchasing habits can lead to a tidal wave of change on the planet. With each mouthful we consume, we influence the future of all life on Earth.

Living humbly and in right relation with all of creation will lead to greater food equity, as those with more resources will make food choices that shift the global food economy in a direction of justice for the entire planet. For so many, eating locally or organically may not be an option due to food deserts and areas of socioeconomic depression that have few options—or none at all—for healthy nourishment. While these spaces have developed from the systemic oppression woven into the fabric of our culture, we can help to change this picture with every purchase we make by committing to make choices that support companies and practices focused on a more humane food system for all. Currently, Rumi and I are blessed to have the space to grow gardens and be able to purchase regeneratively grown animal products from local family farms. When we lived in urban areas, I found local stores and farmers' markets that carried organic and regeneratively grown food, and I grew my own sprouts in jars. Even making small choices to simplify the way we eat—like eating *kitchari*, a nourishing one-pot meal of lentils and grains, regularly—can redirect resources and mindsets to start shifting our food economy in a more just direction.

In addition to supporting our global well-being through more intentional nourishment, this mindset shift also supports the evolutionary upgrade that our bodies undergo in shifting from a carbon to a crystalline structure. As we fully enter fifth-dimensional embodiment, our bodies need simpler, more light-filled food. I'm not prescribing any particular dietary regimen. However, I sense that our Earth would be supported by a collective shift toward a more local, organic way of eating that isn't as heavily dependent on animal products as it has been in the Western world in recent history. As we begin stepping back from a fast-paced lifestyle that leaves many dependent on convenience foods, we can open to a new way, beautifully modeled by the more-than-human realm.

Taking the time to grow a garden, if we have the privilege to do so, can bring us back in touch with the incredible grace that is the creation of food. Going out to harvest wild greens or watching squirrels gathering newly fallen acorns for the winter helps us appreciate the time and energy that goes into the food we eat, and it reminds us that it's worth it to make choices that can help us better nourish ourselves and our world. Better choices will support the interruption of an unsustainable pattern and the conscious creation of a new one, and our individual actions will create a wave of positive change for the collective. The waterways, landscapes, and air polluted from factory farming can be rejuvenated and restored to health by regenerative farming practices rooted in systems of co-creation rather than exploitation.

This is the moment we're in as a global family when we join hands and say yes to a new world, to the best of everything for everyone, and become the awakened humanity we came here to be.

In addition to making conscious choices about what we eat, how we approach nourishment greatly impacts our personal and global experience of life. Infusing our food with love or offering a blessing before we eat enhances the vitality of what we consume and opens us more fully to the alchemy of intentional consumption. The thanks we offer to all those who helped create the food ripples across space and time to uplift those who labored so that we could be fed. If you aren't already doing so, the next time you prepare to eat, you could take a moment to stop and offer gratitude, taking a few deep breaths to honor all of the connections that needed to happen between the millions of microorganisms in the soil, the Sun, the rain, and the hands that were involved in the creation of your food. As you do so, notice the way this elevates the flavors of what you're consuming and the experience of welcoming this prana into your body. Food is medicine, and the blessing of this healing gift can exponentially activate its potency in wonderful ways.

Our lives and our world are created by the ways we nourish ourselves, and integral to this creative process is the digestive fire required to transform anything we ingest into the fuel it becomes for our existence. Our *agni*, Sanskrit for fire and the energy needed for our digestive and metabolic processes, is what allows us to alchemize food and life experiences to create our lives. This creative fire dwells in every living being and is the same fire pulsing at the center of the Earth, her molten core burning at over nine thousand degrees Fahrenheit and erupting as lava that reaches temperatures over sixteen thousand degrees Fahrenheit. This inner fire births new life on Earth and allows us to create new life within our fields of embodiment every time we take something in from our outer environment and transform it into sustenance or a creative offering for the world. The Hawaiian word *mana*, the infinite and eternal power that comes from within, speaks directly to the power we all possess to direct our inner fire in the creative ways we desire. Fire must be fed with fuel, like wood, and the element of oxygen. Similarly, we can stoke our inner fires by feeding them in ways that nourish our agni and by breathing consciously to bring full oxygenation to our systems. In every breath, we can stoke the inner mana and breathe awareness into our ability to reinvent who we are individually and as a collective.

Speaking of fire, Rumi and I just built the first woodstove fire of the season, and we reverently fed it rose petals, tobacco, and lavender that we'd grown and dried as an offering of our gratitude. We can also feed our inner fires with sacred offerings by taking time to pause and breathe before eating to be mindful that our eating benefits our gut biomes, which are integral to our well-being in mind, body, and spirit. When we pause and offer appreciation before eating, we're allowing our nervous systems to come into a state often known as "rest and digest," which is when the body is in a parasympathetic state more conducive to processing and integrating the food we're consuming. Conversely, if we're rushing or stressed, we're likely in a more sympathetic state of arousal, like fight, flight, or freeze, which makes it harder for our bodies to engage in optimal digestive processes. So when we take time to breathe and calm the nervous system before we eat, we're helping our bodies to be more receptive to receiving the nourishment being offered. We're also creating an exchange of energy between our bodies and the food we're consuming that creates an alchemical effect not just on our digestion but on our overall well-being. Over fifty percent of dopamine is produced in the gut, and ninety-five percent of serotonin is made there as well, which influences both mood and physiological wellness, so when we enhance our digestion through mindfulness, we're supporting the healthy flow of these feel-good hormones.

The Earth's microbiome also affects our gut biomes, as the food grown and produced on the Earth's surface directly influences our inner biome when we eat and digest this food. As we've witnessed the Earth's biome diversity decreasing, we've seen a decrease in the human gut biome diversity, which is a direct call to transform farming and agricultural practices into more regenerative methods that focus on increasing biodiversity and contributing to healthy soil and waterways. When we support companies devoted to these practices, bless our food and give thanks, and slow down and chew thoroughly, we begin nourishing ourselves in ways that support our deepest well-being and feed our inner fires. Additionally, exploring mindful eating practices like those outlined in Ayurveda, which views food as medicine, can be an excellent way to learn more about fueling ourselves in ways that enhance our overall wellness in every area of life.

The way we nourish ourselves and our loved ones profoundly impacts all of creation.

By making mindful choices, we can enter a new paradigm of sustenance where all beings are well-fed, and the agricultural and manufacturing practices we support prioritize justice for everyone.

Watching Rumi eat is always a joy because I know that our choices support the world we want to live in and because she so fully savors the sacred pleasure intrinsic to the blessing of true nourishment. May all beings experience the pleasure of having plentiful, healthy food, and may we all receive every mouthful that blesses our journey with gratitude, reverence, and presence.

Through conscious connection with the more-than-human realm that's creating and offering us this nourishment, we begin to reorient ourselves toward an awareness of how our individual choices support the collective well-being of our world. We can see that healthier choices for ourselves also lead to more just food systems for our planet. As a species, we're at a crossroads, and we can turn the tide in how all of creation is cared for by the choices we make in every moment.

At the time of this writing, Pluto has just moved into Aquarius, signaling the beginning of twenty years of profound social transformation and evolutionary breakthroughs in how we sustain and care for ourselves as a planet. We're being invited to direct the power of our privilege in ways that create a positive impact for ourselves and the generations to come, to shift from being unconscious consumers to becoming compassionate creators with every choice we make.

Chapter 10: Ambrosia

Soul Nourishment

Every choice we make affects everything everywhere, so we have the power to create positive change in every moment. What choices are ready for an upgrade in your life? If you release those that no longer feel resonant with your own greatest well-being and that of the planet, which new ones are ready to take their place? If you're interested in making more sustainable consumer choices, what are some action steps that could support this intention? Are there local farmer's markets or artisans whose offerings you're interested in? Are there more responsible companies whose products could support your more conscious lifestyle? If so, what's the next step in exploring these options? Take some space to journal about the habits and patterns you're ready to let go of and about the new and better choices you're ready to welcome in their place. Lastly, offer gratitude to yourself for choosing to make life-affirming choices for the enhanced well-being of all.

CHAPTER 11: ANGELS AND ANCESTORS

"I have come to drag you out of yourself and take you into my heart. I have come to bring out the beauty you never knew you had and lift you like a prayer to the sky."
~Rumi

Three dogs and five years later, I've finally learned how to do birthdays right. Rumi was turning five, which seemed like a milestone, and I cleared the day to devote it to honoring her. The celebrations started the night before, with birthday eve treats, songs, and special playtime. Tucking her in later that night, I felt an even more profound awareness of the vast interconnectedness of this earthly journey as I contemplated all of the synchronicities and alignments that had to occur for her birth and subsequent entrance into my life. As I lay there rubbing her soft ears while she drifted gently into sleep, I offered quiet prayers of appreciation to her mother and father, to all of her canine ancestors who had lived and loved so that she could be with me in this lifetime. In her soft breath on my arm, I felt the breath of all the ones who had come before her. In the welcoming darkness enveloping us as nighttime descended, I felt the presence of all the unseen angels and guides who had been part of the divine orchestration of our sacred union. I felt sweet tears in my eyes as I let myself relax into the soothing energies present with us. I whispered my gratitude into the invisible yet palpable force of love I felt, embracing us with a love that transcended space and time.

When I think about the flow of events that had to occur for Rumi to come into my life, I have complete faith that beneficial energies conspired to bring us together. I frequently communicate with my angels and guides, yet it's rare for me to feel these invisible helpers as tangibly as I did that night of her birthday eve. I interpreted it as an invitation to be even more intentional and open to the magic of the invisible help all around. Sometimes, all that's needed is for me to pause and take a deep breath, look up, and offer a silent "thank you" to feel the powerful presence of the unseen benevolence just waiting to be invited into the moment. My experience has been that these forces of grace—whether we call them angels, ancestors, devas, elementals, or any other name—these more-than-human collaborators want nothing more than to be asked for help, to be welcomed into the aliveness of the living moment. Becoming more intentional in communicating with this love allows us to step into a greater state of conscious co-creation with the vast web of loving kindness available to support us.

Part of living an awakened life is acknowledging this larger field of love that we're a part of, including the different angelic, ancestral, and other beloved ones who support us along the way. I know that I travel with a team of support, and some of my main guides, other than my blood ancestors and the forest energies around me, are the Hawaiian fertility goddess Haumea, the Peruvian goddess Ix Chel, and the late poet Mary Oliver. My days are blessed with conversations and prayers with them, and sometimes, I'm stopped in my tracks when I sense them reaching out and initiating communication with me. Their presence is so real, and the more I feed the connections, the more I feel their support. We're in a time of shifting dimensions, expanding beyond any limiting concepts of reality confined to the realm of three-dimensional existence, and connecting with the unseen forces in our daily experience is a way to nourish this expansion.

You likely have your own unique way of communicating and collaborating with those invisible supporters of your personal journey, which is to be celebrated and nurtured. I connect with my guides throughout the day. Honoring them is part of my morning and evening rituals, and whenever I need a hand, I turn to them and silently invite their guidance, which I feel immediately. Not that I needed "proof" of their presence, but I've definitely received it more times than I can count when Rumi has disappeared into the woods, racing after a herd of deer or some other irresistible wildness. Now, I know she'll always return, but during that first year, when she would be gone far longer than I was comfortable with, the moment I remembered to call upon Basil to bring her back, she would appear. She would race exuberantly down the trail into my waiting arms, a giant smile on her face. Every reappearance would have my heart melting in gratitude and relief while I offered a silent thank you for Basil's constant support. As Anne Lamott says, the three essential prayers are: "help, thanks, and wow," which I've found to be true. There is so much help all around; we only need to remember to slow down long enough to ask for it, giving thanks in advance for the grace that's already on its way.

I believe that living in integrity includes living in a way that honors the labors of our unseen kindred, of our blood ancestors, our "landcestors," and all the more-than-human helpers who are all around. For me, this honoring includes living in a way that will benefit the next seven generations, a principle based on an ancient philosophy of the Haudenosaunee Confederacy (Iroquois), acknowledging that the choices we make now affect life around us and also future generations. The power in this is extraordinary, and in addition to calling us into right action in our daily choices, it's a reminder that we'll also one day be ancestors. How do you want to be remembered for how you helped to shape the world positively for the coming generations?

We have the power right now to become the ones who create a beautiful, healthy future for those who come after us.

Right now, we can internally say *yes* to the invitation to be a force of positive change for the world, to evolve in ways that will light the path for those who are on their way. Involved in this evolutionary shift is a letting go of the ideas of who we thought we were so we can be available for something new; as in any relationship, it's all about connection and the alchemy that happens in that fertile space of presence between the known and the unknown. The ungraspable nature of presence is what, in and of itself, allows us to be open to transformation; as we release ourselves from the limitations of how life has been, we're free to evolve into the next best version of ourselves.

I use the term "landcestors" to refer to the indigenous ones who came before us on whatever sacred land we may be dwelling upon. Honoring the ones who came before us is not only an act of acknowledgment for being on land that was most likely taken unjustly from native peoples but also a way to begin to restore right relationship with the energies of the land and her earlier human caregivers. Daily, I honor the landcestors who came before us in this forest, thanking them and inviting them into collaborative care for the land with me. Opening the lines of communication with the unseen has affirmed to me that there is so much wise, loving help all around and that all we need to begin connecting is to acknowledge this divine presence. Like any relationship, we need to show up, be curious, open-minded, open-hearted, and offer our love. Then, we simply behold the miracle that flowers from the co-creative alchemy that emerges organically.

I've communicated with my angels and guides for as long as I can remember, though when I was young, I didn't have language for it or know that anyone else would understand. It was an internal experience and the closest to what I would have known as prayer. Having been raised in a home where spirituality wasn't discussed, my experience was so personal that I knew intrinsically of its sacredness. I met my first spirit guide when I was four and met him through my beloved beagle, Winky. Now I sense that he was an incarnation of this energy, as my love with Winky is what opened me to the awareness that there's something so much vaster and more beautiful than what's generally acknowledged in modern-day Western culture. As I've grown, I've become more and more aware of the team of support that's always with me, which has shaped my practice of daily communication and co-creation with them. I feel this support with me every day, and even if I forget momentarily, deep down, I know it's there, and this offers profound strength to my spirit.

Haumea is one of these blessed guides; she's an ever-present and loving presence in my life, and her medicine is very much woven into the fabric of this book. Haumea is an ancient Hawaiian fertility goddess revered for her regenerative powers that are known to have made fallow land fertile, brought childbirth to the barren, and restored depleted oceans to ones teeming with abundant life. As one of the primary mother energies, she's known for using her *makalei*, a magic stick, to create seeming miracles out of thin air. Her ability to shapeshift from an elderly woman to a young maiden and back again reflects our capacity to evolve in any moment. She's a powerful guide for all of us as she reminds us of our ability to transform the world around us with heartfelt intentions. Our vibration is our makalei, and it can instantly raise the energies of all with whom we constellate.

Ix Chel is the Mayan goddess of the Moon, love, medicine, gestation, and certain realms of the arts. In hieroglyphics, her name appears as Chak Chel, meaning "large rainbow." Her presence reminds me of the energy we all possess as rainbow bridges between heaven and Earth and the capacity we all carry as medicine-keepers when we embrace and embody our unique soul gifts in community.

My other beloved spirit friend, Mary Oliver, is the gifted poet, dog lover, and queer luminary who changed the world with her beautiful writings about the natural world and the power of presence. Mary came to me early one morning while I was writing by the ocean, the giant orange orb of the Sun just beginning to rise above the shimmering golden horizon. The only others in sight were the seagulls off in the distance and the dolphins playing in the waves before me. Poetry was flowing from my pen, my heart overflowing with love for the exquisite beauty of the moment, when she suddenly came in with diamond-strength presence, her powerful kindness and appreciation for our shared devotion of nature radiating in a sphere of grace all around me. "I'm going to be your mentor," she said. Tears of wonder started flowing down my cheeks at her words, and I smiled in silent agreement. I'd never had a mentor or even thought about having one. Since that day, she's been a constant companion in both my writing journey and my experience of coming into greater harmony with the more-than-human world as part of my evolutionary awakening.

Stones have also been a profound source of guidance and support in my life, as they, too, carry powerful ancestral energies. These ancient ones have been here for thousands, millions, and billions of years, evolving in the Sun and wind to now bless us with their ancient wisdom, and cocreating with crystals and stones is woven into the fabric of my days. In addition to the rocks and crystals I have in my cabin, I love connecting with the stones I encounter in the natural world. Sometimes, when I'm lying on the giant stone by Basil's resting place, my whole being vibrates with the energy emanating from it, not just his but the energy from the millions of years it took for the rock to become what it is now. It likely split off from what used to be a former mountain range that evolved to create the rocky forested hillsides we call home. The river rock around the cabin also radiates ancient wisdom, as a softening of my gaze often reveals tiny fossils mixed in with the smooth stones. Even after years, I'm still in awe each time I find one, the intricate patterns of whorls and ridges telling a story of the ones who blazed the trails for us so many millions of years before. It's miraculous to me that the fossilized remains of our ancestors, the ones who braved this planet when it was largely ocean, are now blessing the space around our home. Holding them in my hand, I can sense the energy of these dear ones who lived and died so we could be here today. If preserved remains reach an age of at least ten thousand years, they become fossils, and some fossils we find today come from as far back as the Archaean Eon, which began almost four billion years ago.

When I open my mind to the reality of being able to be present with that energy, I think of the possibility of someone beholding my fossilized bones and feeling reverence for how our species helped to birth a world of beauty and harmony, one in which someone could be thriving ten thousand years from now on a healthy, vibrant, and abundant Earth. When we open our hearts to the guidance of the more-than-human realm, we can receive the wisdom for bringing this vision into reality, working collaboratively as the multidimensional family of light that we are.

It's pretty much impossible to doubt the presence of this quiet, often invisible help all around—it's so clear that someone, somewhere, is looking out for us. There have been too many unexpected and unique twists and turns in my life to deny that there's a larger, benevolent force overseeing things and lending a helping hand. It's been my experience that the more we acknowledge this support and ask for help, the more it shows up.

The invisible realm loves to be appreciated and recognized, and giving thanks for the blessings, even the tiniest ones, magnetizes more of that frequency into our fields of awareness.

If it feels good, I'd love to invite you to pause and savor a deep breath, offering a silent thank you to all of the unseen energies who've helped you arrive in this moment of your life. If there's something you'd love support with, to invite their help wholeheartedly, offering a wave of gratitude in advance for the grace that's already on its way.

We're so much more powerful than we know, and the root of this power lies in our connection with the sacred energies that are part of the miracle of our existence, not just because they've helped us along the way but because they're an intrinsic part of our lived experience of presence. As I write this, on the last day of summer, as the late afternoon Sun washes the forest in brilliant glowing rays, the warm air is thick with the company of love. Even in the stillness and near silence, I hear and feel the energies of joy, encouragement, and *ohana*, which is Hawaiian for "soul family." "How can I love you best?" I ask the energies I sense in the air around me. "Write about us, invite others to collaborate with us, and open your heart to new ways of cocreating with us. The best is yet to come; this is just the beginning, beloved. Get ready for miracles beyond your wildest dreams. You're being guided, and we'll lead you magnificently. You've been chosen to be here at this pivotal time in Earth's evolution. Ask yourself often, 'What's the best that can happen?' Then, believe it into being. This is what you came here for." I bow my head and inhale deeply; I offer a long, slow breath of gratitude, feeling my ancestors gathered all around me, holding hands and smiling as the Sun sinks gently into the ocean of green.

Our ancestors are a powerful source of care for us in every breath we savor, as they lived and loved so that we could be here in this moment. They're an ever-present force of healing and support, simply waiting to be invited into our experience. This sacred interconnection is supported in our biological makeup by the fact that all the eggs a woman will ever carry form in her ovaries while she is a four-month-old fetus in the womb of her mother. This means our cellular life as an egg begins in the womb of our grandmothers. Each of us spent five months in our grandmother's womb, and she, in turn, formed within the womb of her grandmother. I can't help but smile in wonder every time I think about that as I feel the sacred presence of all the ones who came before me, pulsing love through my heartbeat here and now.

There are surges in potentiality when we come together intentionally with these unseen helpers and guides because the effect of these connections is exponential. When we attune to the profoundly kind energies of support around us, we alter the quantum wave structure of our known reality and create new harmonics of love that radiate out and affect all of creation. When someone once asked me how to connect with our unseen companions, my reply was to open the heart. Whichever way you're inspired to communicate and co-create is valid—simply listening is a beautiful gateway into sensing these invisible friends. In the practice of two-way prayer, one is invited to offer one's prayers or intentions and then maintain a space of deep listening, which is sometimes necessary for receiving the guidance and blessings being offered back. Sometimes, I like to create more ceremonial space for this communication. I clear the space by cleaning and smudging with Palo Santo or sweetgrass, ringing a bell or crystal bowl, playing the drum, using my voice to sing or tone, or lighting a candle. It's not necessary, though sometimes it helps center the space for the frequency of communication I desire. Any way you're called to connect with these dear ones is beautiful, and the results will always be only supportive. Mahalo, beloved ancestors, landcestors, angels, and guides. Your loving kindness is a blessing for which I am infinitely and eternally grateful.

Chapter 11: Angels and Ancestors

Soul Nourishment

How are you honoring and cocreating with the larger field of love around you? Do you feel your angels and ancestors close, and if so, what do you notice when you invite them into conversation and communion with you? Take a moment to journal about any guidance or words of encouragement that you hear from them. Knowing that you will one day be an ancestor, ask yourself how you want to be remembered for how you helped to shape the world positively for the coming generations. Allow yourself to dream big and imagine yourself as the best version of yourself, fulfilling your soul's greatest intentions. When you're finished, offer thanks in advance for the sacred support of the unseen helpers and guides all around you, cocreating this vision with you in every moment.

CHAPTER 12: BREATH

"Only from the heart can you touch the sky."
~Rumi

There are few sounds I love more than the sound of Rumi's breathing while she's sleeping. The sweet, gentle rhythm emanates such a deep sense of calm and safety that it naturally evokes those feelings in me. I love to lie down beside her in the evening after she's gone to bed, my arms around her as I rest there smiling, feeling the soft puff of air on my arm as she exhales, and feeling the sense of complete surrender in the slow, steady rising and falling of her warm body. Like heaven on Earth, it feels like a peak moment every time. Sometimes, I wake in the middle of the night and hear the peaceful sound of her breath, the soothing cadence of her in deep slumber in the quiet stillness, and it's like a lullaby for my soul. I'll lie in bed with my heart melting in love; hearing your baby's breath, knowing they're safe and held in the peace of rest, is pure holiness.

Equally swoon-worthy is the sound of her dreaming, hearing her barely audible musings while her paws move purposefully, racing about heroically in her private dreamscape. I only wake her if it sounds like it's distressing, wrapping my arms around her little body and soothing her with assurances of her safety and my presence. In those moments, I feel our connection fully with each other and the divine. Sometimes, in those sacred spaces, I feel myself as the divine, smiling upon the exquisite beauty of creation and feeling a love in my heart so deep and vast that all I can do is revel in its pure presence. And it's in this, in the invitation into true presence, that grace arrives. It comes in like a spring breeze from deep in the forest valley and sweeps me off my feet, lifting me into a frequency of love that instantly transforms everything. This is remembrance, and I've found that one of the most potent and effective ways for me to reach this portal of awakening is through the breath itself.

Breathing with Rumi while she sleeps is a profound pleasure, deepening my reverence for the miracle of breath that sustains our existence. I call it a "miracle" not only because the subtle essence that animates us—the life force of the Universe—is carried by the oxygen we breathe, reminding us with each breath of our eternal power and our mortality, but also because of the beautiful way breath weaves us all into a living web of aliveness. All of creation is breathing the same air, and as we potentiate our exhales with our intentions and charge the molecules with our energy, we're sharing that love with all beings.

With every breath, we're contributing our unique essence and light to the global field of consciousness, and we're breathing in the love being offered.

Right now, there are so many souls who are intending for good, who are meditating and offering love, who are breathing in appreciation for life, and who are sending this gratitude out from their hearts. Every time I pause to remember this, to think of the millions of humans who are in some kind of prayer or another state of mindfulness intending to generate *metta*, loving kindness, for all beings, my heart opens in even deeper awe and wonder, and I direct my intention to the love being offered on my own exhale.

While everyone might not be focused on the upliftment of the world, there are so many who are, and love is so much more powerful than anything less than that. The more we focus on this, the more we choose to become part of the blessing, part of the grace being breathed through us and out into the atmosphere, and the more we awaken to our collaborative power as co-creators of a new paradigm. There is so much power in the breath to create change in our personal ecosystems and the larger ecosystem to which we're all contributing. It's fascinating, this blessing that we're all receiving, this magical life force that our bodies naturally know how to take in through the multitude of processes happening through our respiratory systems, and even more impressive is that all of this continues happening even when we're not conscious of it and while we're sleeping. Just as inspiring is how we can help each other in this process, inviting deeper breaths together and expanding our capacity to breathe more fully and generate healing within and around us.

Chapter 12: Breath

As we become more aware of our breath, we make ourselves more available to the higher consciousness on offer through the art of breathing.

We're becoming light beings, Homo Luminous, as the planet is bathed in new frequencies of light from the Sun being channeled from the galactic center, the heart of our galaxy.

Much of the process of evolving from a carbon to a crystalline state of embodiment is happening through breathing in the light that's being transcoded through the photosynthetic grace of green plants, which is then released into the atmosphere for us to receive. As we inhale it into our bodies, it's filtered through our loving awareness and back out in an ascending spiral of awakening consciousness, moving into greater harmony as this loop of reciprocity continues. If it feels good, you could experiment with it right now, intending to inhale well-being and breathe out blessings for all; if you're outside or near a plant, you could explore opening your heart to the living energy around it, intending to receive the love being offered. If it feels supportive, you could explore setting an intention to breathe this way throughout your day or night and watch miracles unfold, both in your lived experience and in your consciousness. I love breathing with trees, flowers, birds, and the Moon. I imagine our breath entraining, and I give thanks, knowing that my system is regulating with the energy of the more-than-human ones breathing with me in this field of resonance and blessing.

As I wrote that last sentence, I was inspired to take a deep, conscious inhale, which almost always brings a smile to my face. As much as I intend to breathe fully and consciously, I sometimes forget, and the immediate relief from remembering to take a full breath is pure delight. A dear friend and mentor once said that a good goal in life is to breathe diaphragmatically almost 24/7. This means breathing fully and completely from the diaphragm so the belly is soft and round on the inhale and flattens back toward the spine on the exhale. This allows the body to breathe in the way it's designed to, resulting in our bodies functioning more efficiently and tapping into greater well-being, both in the moment and over the long term. There are, of course, times when one might want and need to breathe in another way; however, the overall vision of complete diaphragmatic breathing for most of the day is usually a wonderful intention. So perhaps as you read, you might hold an intention for deep, full belly breathing, allowing the tonic of full oxygenation to open your neural pathways and bring fresh prana into your bloodstream and brain. This seemingly subtle shift in embodiment will lead to profound shifts in existence, helping to repair and rejuvenate tissues and organs and soothing and grounding the nervous system in many beneficial ways.

Further inspiration for breath awareness came from my meditation teacher asking, "How smooth, even, and calm can my next breath be?" This is incredibly supportive in any moment when I'm feeling off-center, as it brings my focus back to my breath and allows my mind to let whatever it was ruminating on drift into the background, still accessible for processing yet secondary to the focus of keeping my breath full and complete. This allows the mental body to relax its narrow focus on what might be considered a "problem," and the deeper oxygen flow can allow for greater awareness and potential solutions that may have been inaccessible when being overly fixated on the issue at hand.

As Einstein said, "A problem can't be solved at the level at which it was created," meaning that we must soften our mental grip to let in the more expansive, imaginative energies that can lift us into the realm of new possibilities. The mind follows the breath, and the body follows the mind, so if we can maintain deep, regulating breaths, the mind will naturally follow this energy flow. The body will follow the mind, bringing all our beingness into a greater connection with the larger field of creative intelligence. Whatever practice centers you and brings you into presence is both the gateway and the destination, and when we realize this, we can soften into the reality that every breath offers the potential to be in divine awareness, to be in a state of oneness with the greater benevolence breathing and connecting us all.

Everything is breathing together all the time, and the more-than-human realm is continually inviting us into greater awareness of breath simply because it welcomes us to slow down and behold a hawk flying through the sky or to witness the silence of the cedars in winter. One conscious breath can bring us more fully into the body, relax the mind, and open the heart to the loving guidance that's always present, within and all around.

Chapter 12: Breath

The breath of essence is the subtle mother of all of creation, and the more we attune to this flow of aliveness within our bodies, the more we allow our consciousness to be inspired and expanded by the vast ocean of love that is its very source.

Breath is the life-giving elixir of Source that allows the living world to collaborate in a continual exchange of oxygen and carbon dioxide that nourishes, heals, and sustains life as we know it. On one level, breath is the reception and expulsion of air in the lungs, and it provides eighty percent of the metabolic energy we need for our existence, while twenty percent comes from the food we consume. It's the very substance that allows us to be alive; the word "spirit" is derived from the Latin word for "breath," *spiritus*, illustrating that breath gives us life and carries within it so much more than just the elemental components it contains. Prana is the subtle life force that animates everything in the known Universe and is carried on the breath—the basic building block for all of existence. With this awareness, every breath is a prayer, enlivening us with divinity.

As we step into the Symbiocene Era focused on harmonious coexistence, something magnificent is happening, and we're being invited to collaborate and celebrate it together. The new Earth is already here and alive in some places, people, and fields of aliveness. Spaces—between thoughts, ideas, breaths, and actions—are some of the most fertile and magical cauldrons of life. Perhaps we're in one giant space between the ages right now. To enter into the void, the space of all that's possible, a letting go of the past must happen to open ourselves to something so much more aligned and nourishing for the new and the now. Breath allows us to explore the power of creating and exploring space within, suspending thought, releasing energy, and allowing something new to shape our reality.

We're one living consciousness being breathed, and we have the ability in every moment to saturate the world with the love-infused air we're offering up.

We're in a global heart-opening that's being supported by the human and more-than-human kindred souls breathing with us right now. Right now, countless beings are chanting, praying, sending healing light, envisioning peace, and believing in miracles. We can open ourselves to this grace, receiving its love and sending it back into creation. We become what we believe, and our beliefs bring new possibilities into being. Believe in people, in this incredible Earth, in this brilliant Universe, and in the consciousness we share and shape with every intentional breath. The principle of Makia, "energy goes where attention flows," reminds us that we see the world we seek. The world is as we perceive it. Right now, we can cocreate miracles; right now, we can open up to grace.

The first time I remember having an experience of feeling myself opening up to this infinite grace was when I was practicing the Ha breath with my *kumu*, which is Hawaiian for "teacher." I was at his cozy, welcoming home, lying on his healing table while he was gently guiding me to focus on this simple and powerful exhale-focused breath practice. It's intended to bring one into greater awareness of the power of combining breath and intention and inspiring responsibility for the creative force being exhaled into the Universe. Both calming to the mind and soothing to the soul, it invites us to more fully embody our potential to shape the world with each breath. After a few minutes of lying there with my eyes closed and feeling the breath building in my system, I had an awareness of him gently pulling his energy away from me, simply holding space while I deepened into my experience of surrendering more fully into the breath. Suddenly, my perception shifted, and I had what I can only describe as one of the most incredible experiences of my life. All awareness of myself as a separate human form dissolved, and I felt myself embodied as Pele, the active volcano on the island where I was living. My whole being was alive in this energy and form, and I witnessed with awe as the breath carried me through a visceral experience of being immersed in this frequency of mythical volcanic form.

As I surrendered more fully into the flow of energy, I then felt myself transform into the ocean. I again surrendered in wonder as I felt the bodily sensations of being the sea in form and vibration, which then evolved into beholding myself metamorphosing into the vastness of the sky, feeling all limitations of my concept of self vanish as I exhaled into the complete freedom of unbounded space. Tears flowed down my face as I allowed the most profound sense of calm and bliss to wash through my energy field, the breath carrying me deeper and deeper into the reality of our infinite nature and potential to experience our oneness with all of creation. Gently, he guided me back into my body and the safe space we were in, and my breath softly returned to its normal flow as I slowly opened my eyes to a whole new perspective of the world. That sacred exchange opened me up to a profound awareness of how the breath connects us to everything, and the infinite potential we all possess to experience and embody the power and divinity within the vastness of creation. I had a visceral awareness of the collective messiah we are and how the breath is the creative medium with which we can begin to birth a new world. I began consciously breathing with the trees, the clouds, the Moon, my pups, and anyone with whom I felt soul alignment, and it shifted what had felt like a perpetual sense of separation within me, a low-level hum in the background that I had accepted as part of reality. It was replaced with a sense of interconnection with all of life that felt like true safety, peace, and homecoming within, what D. R. Butler calls "the oasis of the present moment."

When the wild honeysuckle came into bloom this spring, it opened a new dimension of awareness to this oasis accessible through the breath. Every time I walked by, I was drawn to offer my whole being to the magnificence of her intoxicating scent, closing my eyes as I inhaled deeply, over and over and over, the aliveness permeating deeper into my lungs and heart with every delicious draw. The scent only seemed to get better as the days went on. I found myself taking sprigs wherever I went so that I could breathe it through the day, the combination of sweetness and wild earthiness alchemizing in a sensory experience that left me smiling in wonder and inhaling with that same depth of delight even when I wasn't near the fragrant blossoms.

We can consciously enhance our ability to breathe more fully, engaging with the gift of breath in new ways.

By directing oxygen to areas in the body and mind that need healing and allowing ourselves the gift of a complete exhale, we can settle our systems and soothe our minds. Developing our breath capacity is free, almost always available, and can lead to profound shifts, not only because of the ways it enhances our personal well-being but because of the ways it brings us into deeper awareness of breathing with all of creation and shaping reality with the love we're exhaling into the world.

Plant medicine can be a beautiful support on this journey of remembering and awakening, and the most ecstatic and accessible plant medicine in the world is oxygen. It opens our neural pathways, oxygenates our blood, facilitating well-being in every aspect of our experience, and it can both enliven or calm the nervous system depending on what is needed. Breath (and laughter) are truly the best medicines. Sometimes, I feel like my real job is to be in nature, breathing out my love-infused CO_2 to share with the living world around me. If all humans were to intend for a day, even for part of a day, to breathe that way, a new world would manifest. The subtle energy of prana that is carried in the air and in the breath is a living substance with the power to communicate vibrationally with all the other prana circulating in our world.

Bringing awareness into form, spirit into matter, and intention into our breath makes us all alchemists.

This sweetest of alchemies, the ability to infuse prana with blessings that will become the fabric of the living world, allows us in every breath to contribute beauty to the creation of the new Earth.

It's all a journey of interconnection and remembrance that fills my heart with gratitude and peace. The breeze in the trees is happening because of the air wafting through the branches; that same air is filling my lungs with life force, and that life force was once sunlight that was transformed into oxygen through the magnificence of photosynthesis carried out by the tree leaves that are being sustained by the carbon dioxide I'm breathing out. We're all in this together, and when I breathe into that, I'm filled with such faith that my heart opens even wider. These moments of awareness, however brief, change us forever, and they change the world.

Anytime you're blessed to remember to take a conscious breath in connection with the living world, realize that you're contributing more beauty to this precious world than you may ever know.

This is the invisible and incredible power we all possess as carriers of the sacred source of divinity—the breath. Because we're all fractals of

Source and unique expressions of the divine, our uniqueness is precisely what allows us to live in integrity, to live as an integral part of the whole.

When we see our three-leggedness not as a problem but as essential to the miracle, we can love ourselves unconditionally. When we slow down and turn within so that we come face-to-face with our soul, our original face of the divine, we're able to see all others through this lens, and we can explore being alive together in ways that we couldn't have seen when looking through the eyes of separation. "If thine eye be single" is a reference to the awakening of the third eye, an energy center located slightly above and between the eyebrows, and the accompanying ability to see as the divine sees. Viewing ourselves as both individual and whole simultaneously is the expansion of consciousness we're in the midst of. We're remembering how to soften our edges enough to experience our interconnectedness while also appreciating the beauty of our unique offerings to the collective. In every breath, we're awakening from the dream of unworthiness to the reality of our innate value and all of existence. We're embracing our three-leggedness not as a limitation but as the gateway to creating the world of harmony and loving kindness we all long to experience. As the poet Rumi wrote, "Come, come, whoever you are. Wanderer, worshiper, lover of leaving. It doesn't matter. Ours is not a caravan of despair. Come, even if you have broken your vows a thousand times. Come, yet again, come." No matter what your past has entailed or how you may have judged yourself or the world, your next breath is an affirmation of your greatness, of our shared divinity, and of the invitation to come again, to start afresh, right now, in the blessing of this very breath.

As I was writing, I offered a deep breath of gratitude out into the forest surrounding me as I asked, "How can I love you best?" I heard, "You have to surrender everything you thought you knew about love, life, and how it will go. We will show you a world that you have only dreamed of. Keep believing in it; it's happening, and you're creating it in this very moment. There are new states of consciousness that you're receiving through the breath. Keep breathing and continue opening. We'll guide you wisely, always." I paused, breathing silently in gratitude. I felt a fresh window of awareness open while witnessing the oxygen traveling deep into my lungs, activating new dimensions of aliveness in every molecule of my being, bowing to the love that is life.

Breath is a gateway to transformation. We're literally breathing new life into our minds and hearts with every inhale and clearing space for this new life with every exhale.

To be open to new ways of being, we must first soften our limitations around what we think is possible.

We can do this by breathing through the heart with the intention of allowing the mind and heart to merge. This opens us to the magic of the *nous*, the vision of the soul, in which our mind is informed by the loving awareness of the heart. This concept of the mind isn't a dualistic idea of a mind separate from the body; it involves our whole being as a way of interpreting the world within and around us. The Mary Magdalene Gospels describe the nous as a portal to truly embody the divine love that we're here to be. Thomas Merton describes the heart as "a pure diamond, blazing with the invisible light of heaven," beautifully capturing the infinitude of grace that's always breathing within each of our hearts. The separation is an illusion; love is here right now, breathing as you, enlivening you, transfiguring you into a being of light as you allow the life-giving oxygen to deeply nourish your cells while exhaling your gratitude even more fully to the living world.

This breath contains infinitudes, and you have been chosen as its precious and beloved recipient.

Right now, you and I are connecting as two souls alive in this present moment. Though I wrote these words in a moment before you're reading them, our energies are aligning beyond the bounds of time and space. This text is light-encoded so that we're meeting soul to soul, my loving awareness meeting yours, breathing life into these words together as you welcome them into your consciousness.

Love is alive, and by directing our energy to the vibration of creative potential in this living moment, we're enhancing the well-being of the Universe.

How full, deep, and life-affirming can your next breath be? Allow yourself this blessing, and as you do, know that you're offering it to all of creation.

Chapter 12: Breath

Soul Nourishment

When it feels supportive to your system, try exploring any or all of these breath practices, taking space to journal about how you feel before and after each one, and giving thanks for the gift of breath uniting us all.

- **Cyclic sighing:** Breathe deeply into the belly and then follow it with a second inhale, taking in as much air as possible, and then exhale slowly with your lips pursed like you're breathing out through a straw, extending the exhale as long as is comfortable for up to five minutes.
- **Diaphragmatic breathing:** Breathe fully and deeply into the belly, letting the belly expand out on the inhale and soften back toward the spine on the exhale.
- **Presence breathing:** Watching the breath and intentionally breathing in peace and breathing out love.
- **Coherent breathing:** Breathe long, deeply, and smoothly with the intention of taking as few breaths per minute as possible.
- **Nadi Shodhana:** There are many ways to practice this alternate-nostril breath technique, and it helps to balance the left and right hemispheres of the brain and bring the lunar and solar aspects of the energy body into balance. Begin by connecting with the breath and gently closing the right nostril with your thumb, inhaling through the left nostril, then closing the left nostril with your little or ring fingers. Open and exhale slowly through the right nostril. Keep the right nostril open, inhale, then close it, and open and exhale slowly through the left. This is one cycle. Repeat three to five times, then release the hand and return to normal breathing. Many variations of this

practice can be explored in greater depth and offer a diversity of support for the system.

- **Ha breath:** This breath involves a deep, full inhale through the nose and a strong, powerful exhale of the sound "ha" through an open mouth.

CHAPTER 13: PRESENCE

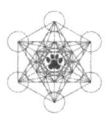

"There is a voice that doesn't use words. Listen."
~Rumi

Winter came early this year, the temperatures plunging below zero before the final orange-gold leaves had fallen from the trees. We knew the cold was coming, and we stockpiled firewood outside the front door and lit the woodstove before the first snowflakes began to fall. That night, as we sat in front of the warm blaze, the flames dancing an enchanting poetry of heat and aliveness, I fell into one of the most blissful states I'd ever experienced, what D. R. Butler calls "the rapture of being fully present." As the temperatures slowly dropped and the snow began to pile up in soft ridge lines along the windowsills, Rumi and I cuddled in close in front of the fire, her warm body snug and surrendered in the circle of my arms, soaking in the heat and savoring my love. I felt myself being lulled into deeper and deeper bliss as I felt her peaceful breath against my skin, the warmth of our bodies melting together in deep contentment, and the sweet sense of safety and home that I felt radiating from deep in our bones.

The absolute pleasure and healing that followed as I allowed myself to let go into the grace of that moment completely is deeply imprinted in my awareness, as it initiated me to another dimension of presence as a greater benevolence filled my consciousness. Presence can be understood as the indescribable peace of being in attunement with the reality of life exactly as it is. For me, mindfulness is a welcoming gateway to the blessing of the living moment, as it can welcome a softening of the mind that makes us more fully available for the miracle of the now. This presence is available in every moment, and mindfulness practices like meditation have greatly enhanced my ability to inhabit this state of awareness. Blessedly, the more I practice, the more these portals of presence appear in my world.

One of my peak meditation experiences happened early one winter morning. It was still dark out, and the fresh snowfall had brought a soft hush to the forest. A single candle lit; I was deep in reverence as I sat silently before the frost-edged window in front of the altar. As I dropped further into the sacred silence, my calm exploded in a cascade of uncontrollable laughter when Rumi suddenly leaped at me from behind and began furiously whipping me on the back with her new stuffed pig in an irresistible invitation to play. My laughter elevated as she began enticing me with her adorable growls and meows, intermingled with loud squawks from the multi-squeakered pig. My heart burst open in the perfection of being fully alive and present with the divine through the pure joy of Rumi and her pig. It was an exquisite reflection of the reality that mindfulness is available in every moment of life and is only enhanced by inviting in the aliveness that's all around. She brought increased joy and appreciation into the moment. I felt our molecules of delight dancing together and enlivening the field around us with such devotion that the room was practically glowing.

Every moment, whether in sacred silence or holy squeaking play, is an invitation to the magic of presence.

The seen and unseen grace offered from all around can light our trail to the ever-loving, ever-wise space of presence, and as Rumi suggests, inviting it in through communion with our beloved animal companions is a fantastic way to practice.

As the Hawaiian teaching around grace receiving gratitude invites, we can offer gratitude even if we can't yet see the outcome, as offering our thanks in advance invokes the grace we desire. I love this orientation as a way of practicing mindfulness, of being so present as to embrace the mystery of each moment with full faith in the goodness guiding it. I began an intentional mindfulness practice in my early twenties, and since that first morning, breathing deeply as I sat silently before the rising Sun, I've rarely missed a day. It didn't take long for me to realize the tremendous impact a morning meditation practice had on the rest of my day, and it continues to enhance my ability to be present to the beauty of life within and around me in ways that transcend words.

Mornings have always held a contemplative energy for me. I love witnessing the sky turn from dark to light, hearing the first sounds of the wild ones awakening, and savoring the energy of a fresh start in the new day dawning. Since Rumi came into my world, my delight in mornings has made a quantum leap, as our days now start with cuddles, kisses, and songs. The following hours are blessed with playtime, treats, and plenty more cuddles and kisses amidst my morning practice, work, and the endless and wonderful homesteading tasks. Since my first taste of meditation in my twenties, I've intentionally crafted space for mindfulness to align my energy for the new day. My practice has had the same basic elements for over two decades: meditation and writing. Grounding my energy and focusing my mind in meditation opens a channel for my writing practice, often a conversation with the unseen realm of support around me that helps me create the day ahead. Whether it's writing or any other creative endeavor, a practice of connecting to the divine within by allowing the mind to settle and the heart to open can be fertile nourishment for the brilliance within to rise above the mental chatter that can distract us from engaging and expressing the deeper wisdom of the soul. Even if the time I have available is brief, savoring even a few moments of this presence and connection is a super tonic for the day.

As I write, I pause to look up and smile at the golden sunlight filtering through the early November forest; most of the leaves have fallen, yet the light sparkles like diamonds on the few still hanging. The hillside is opening up, and I can see the distant pine ridge emerging on the horizon. Change is in the air, and there's an invitation to stillness, to breathe and be present with the beauty of transition all around me. Words are bubbling up in my mind, yet I resist the urge to write them down. Instead, I breathe deeply of the cold, clear air and savor the warm sunbeam shining down on my forehead. This is what it feels like to live, to soften my belly as I witness the strands of a spider web glistening in the light as the rustle of the autumn breeze inspires a deeper inhale and a slow smile to spread across my face. Will there be another moment like this?

I'm here now, both receiving and offering, grace receiving gratitude, internally bowing in awe as I simultaneously let go of everything to be present in the unspeakable beauty of the now. Thank you to the love that has brought me to this holiness and the desire in my heart to share it with you. Wherever you are, may you feel the exquisite peace of the divinity of this wild and beautiful forest breathing through you as it now breathes through me, uniting our hearts across miles and timelines to come together in this eternal here and now. In this holy intimacy, we remember and awaken to the larger truth of our sacred union as kindred souls who've chosen to incarnate together to birth something extraordinary through the power of our heart's presence. As I was writing, a hawk flew low and slow through the trees to land on a branch to my right, her plush feathered body gliding silently through the shimmering leaves. There's magic all around, and it comes alive when we attune to the magic within, magnetizing that which is a vibrational match through our mindful awareness and anchored presence.

Rumi helps to bring me into greater mindfulness because of the tremendous love I share with her, and part of my capacity to experience this love is because I've created room in my life to be more present with her than I have with my previous canine companions. This depth of presence has been transformative because it's created space for love to enter so deeply into my consciousness that it's evolved how I orient myself in the world. It began with my relationship with Rumi and has expanded to influence how I interact with everyone I encounter. When I feel distracted and needing to come into presence, I remember that my attention is my makalei, the magic wand of Haumea's that creates miracles simply by the direction of its attention and intention. When we come into presence, we come into conscious collaboration with something so much bigger than our individual plans and perspectives.

When we're present, we aren't entangled in the past or the future, and we're more open to the vast wisdom contained in this state of openness that can lead to quantum shifts in our awareness.

Our presence is our attention, one of our most extraordinary powers. Rumi brings me into greater presence through the love and joy she brings to almost everything she does, as even the simplest acts become celebrations for her. Even more powerful is the way she, like all beings in the more-than-human realm, embodies aliveness. This presence draws me out of my head and into the wholeness of the moment, enhancing my embodied awareness. I sense that the greatest gift the more-than-human realm is offering is this mirroring of presence—an invitation to connect with the divine intelligence infusing every moment.

Presence allows us to be open for the not-yet-imagined, and when we quiet the mind for the subtle, soft voice of the soul to be heard, it's always there, patient and kind in the stillness within. The global awakening that's happening is reorienting us to this ever-loving internal wisdom within. When we're centered here in our connection to Source, we can breathe in something so powerful and transformative that how we perceive, make meaning of, and understand ourselves and our world evolves. This is the shift in consciousness being brought in by the Age of Aquarius.

We're evolving to see our interconnectedness while being centered in our individual connections with the divine, which are the source of the unique blessings we're here to contribute.

The *Tao*, or the way, is unknowable, yet it's deeply known within the very fabric of our awareness. In research, the term "warm data" relates to the unmeasurable, which can only be understood by being present with the world around and observing and sensing the energetic exchanges that the ancients knew were often the truest source of information. Much of humanity has become accustomed to left-brain-dominant thinking, devoted to the dogmatism of science and data, and we're now moving back into balance by creating space for the intuitive, more feminine ways of knowing. This balance brings us into presence with a higher harmony of awareness that inspires choices supportive of the good of all beings, which is true wisdom.

We can come into presence by inviting our physical bodies to relax, loosening our jaws and lower backs, and feeling the eyes and the breath begin to relax more fully. As we allow this softening, we may notice space beginning to appear between our thoughts. It's in this sacred in-between space that wisdom and grace can arise. To create something new, we have to think in new ways and create internal space for new insights to come in.

Practicing presence through meditation or any other avenue that works for you is a way to consciously invite the divine into your awareness to cocreate more consciously with this force of supreme love. Presence is our doorway into now. "Now"…what a concept; it's the space that contains everything and the only time that ever really exists. All we have is now, the portal for our awakening.

In some ways, the journey of awakening is one of simplifying ourselves and meeting life as it is. When we let go of trying to make life conform to our agenda about how it should be, we can awaken to the life that's here waiting to be savored by us. We've likely had many moments of awareness when we looked back and saw that everything was divinely orchestrated, even the things we may have thought we didn't want, because they all got us here, to the only reality, overflowing with miracles and possibilities. It took over thirteen billion years for us to get to this moment. With a deep exhale, we can practice letting it all go, inviting ourselves into the beauty of this living moment free of expectations or limiting ideas of how life might appear. This is one of my favorite mindfulness practices: To be aware of how much has happened to bring me to this moment and then exhale and release it with gratitude to open my consciousness to the wild and fertile richness of the now.

What else is possible?

Asking myself this as I look up to the bright blue sky, to the elegantly swaying treetops, I feel my thoughts pausing to create space for blessings I can't even begin to imagine, and I breathe into this, giving thanks in advance for the grace that's already on its way.

The spiritual world holds amazing mysteries and ineffable beauty, as the three-dimensional reality is not the only reality, and presence itself has no physical form. The mind is just a tiny particle in the field of awareness, and coming into spaces of loving awareness allows us to expand beyond limited concepts of our personal and collective potential for existence. Coming into this presence enables us to live from coherence, a sense of inner alignment with our humanity and our divinity, and when living from here, to take the risk of telling a new story. Exploring the power of presence on our evolutionary journey allows us to hone the art of directing our intention and attention. When we invite our will into this collaboration, we can relax in the security of trusting in the larger benevolence supporting us. We remember that we aren't ever working alone, that, in fact, our will and divine will are working in concert, clearing the way for as-of-yet-unknown solutions and unexpected blessings. The more-than-human world guides us in remembering how to live from this place of presence. As we do, we release the outworn perceptions of separation and open ourselves to the interconnected, all-possible nature of now. Everything is evolving, and while it may seem like things are speeding up in this process, the way through is often supported by slowing down and coming into the space of connecting heart to heart with the larger force of love all around.

This process allows us to decenter ourselves and begin comprehending the truth of our interbeingness with all of creation and the quantum potential of reality.

While my spiritual practice has been a guiding light for much of my life, it was a mostly solitary journey until recently. I read many mystical teachings and studied different philosophies aligned with my eco-mystical heart. I shared terrific conversations with kindred spirits and sometimes attended various gatherings. Still, it wasn't until I moved out to the forest that I began a regular practice with other humans. At the time of this writing, I'm part of a circle of beautiful companions who gather every morning from all over the world, thanks to technology, to breathe and meditate with the loving guidance of our teacher. There's something so powerful about coming together in shared service to a greater vision; in this case, the greater vision is universal. Our morning practice has opened me even more deeply to the power of two or more gathering with a shared intention, and it's invited me to broaden my exploration of this co-creative potency with the more-than-human realm.

What's been growing in me as I deepen my practice is an expanded awareness of the subtle realms of reality and the beauty contained in this living field of consciousness. The inner landscape is a vast and infinite space of loving kindness and sacred wisdom, and the more I get in touch with this ever-present grace within, the more empowered I become as the creatrix of my reality. I'm witnessing my own divination process, the spiritualization of matter happening through my focus and intention to more fully embody the light of kindness we all are. Those around me may feel that there's been no noticeable outward change in me, but inwardly, tectonic shifts have occurred.

Soon after beginning this shared practice, I noticed the sudden absence of thinking I needed anything external to make me okay. After years of harboring a vague sense that something outside of me—another person, plant medicine, a job, or location—would bring me greater well-being, I remembered that true wellness comes from inner alignment with my divinity. The shift was subtle yet profound. Though my orientation has shifted, I still love people, wonderful environments, and beautiful plants. I feel myself rooted in something more eternal and reliable, which is the unchanging love within that's been with me long before I came into this earthly body and will be with me long after it's gone. For the first time, I understood what it felt like to embody peace. I know what bliss is when I pause long enough to breathe into this state of presence with the love within. It's available in every moment because it's who we are beyond any of the stories we may engage in. Our *sadhana*, our spiritual practices, help us cultivate these experiences so that we begin to notice them more frequently, which then magnetizes more of them to us. Our sadhana can look like anything: Washing the dishes, taking care of our babies, cooking for another, sitting in meditation, or walking in the woods; it doesn't matter what it is because ultimately, all of life is sadhana, and when we live in this way as if everyone and everything is holy, miracles happen. There is something so vast and so benevolent that's created us all, and that something is the love that's writing this very sentence and is the same love in you that's reading it.

This universal current of grace is coursing through every molecule of creation.

When we direct our attention to it, we enliven its presence in our consciousness, embodying it more fully and transforming the world through the blessing of soul resonance. Whether practicing with others or singularly, when we center in this inner grace and focus our energy on peace, miraculous shifts occur individually and universally.

How can we direct our presence to be a bridge between ancient wisdom and our emergent future? We can invite it to soften our limiting perceptions of reality and open us to new ways of living in greater integrity with each other.

Presence welcomes us into alignment with all of life because as we become more open to new possibilities, we become inspired to live from a frequency of loving kindness.

Our more-than-human guides support this awakening in us as they model presence and loving kindness in powerfully wise ways. We're shifting our focus from surviving to thriving, to understanding why we're all here, to the awareness of dwelling in a love so vast words can't contain it. This love is taking care of everything, the things we aren't yet clear about and the questions whose answers we're still living into, and working with this larger field of intelligence requires building our spiritual muscles of patience and faith. We need the times that bring us to our knees in prayer and that keep us in awe of the mystery because they show us the power of how we focus our attention. As we allow our faith in this unseen grace to grow, we notice the glimmers of miracles appearing more and more frequently, and we, in turn, begin to give thanks more regularly and in advance. We begin to witness ourselves being carried in a river of kindness, and as we relax back into this gentle aliveness, the softening occurs.

The space between thoughts, breaths, and the known and unknown is a sacred and fertile space for awakening and remembrance.

As we become more aware of these holy portals of potential, we more fully embody our boundless creative power to anchor in new frequencies of love for all of existence.

Soul Nourishment

In what areas of your life do you feel most present? Are there places you wish you could embody this state of awareness more fully? If so, explore bringing the intention of conscious breathing into your experience in those spaces and witness any shifts that occur. What is your current sadhana? Does it feel fulfilling to you on a soul level? Are there elements you'd like to evolve or add to your current practices that would more deeply support your visions of your most authentic life?

Take space to journal about these, noting how your past practices have supported you in getting to this moment and celebrating both who you are now and who you are becoming, breathing deeply and giving thanks for all that has been and all that will be.

INVITATION

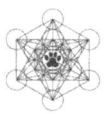

"Set your life on fire. Seek those who fan your flames."
~Rumi

Thank you for going on this journey with us. We're writing a really good new story, and we're being invited to evolve our beliefs about ourselves and the world around us. Everything is energy; our thoughts are energy in motion, and we have the opportunity to dream in a new and better iteration of reality. What's the best that can happen? Right now, we can soften our hearts, relax our bodies, and savor a deep breath. Presence with the breath allows us to connect with the source of all life and the foundation of our well-being. Reality begins to shift when we breathe with this greater field of awareness and envision a just world. Where two or more are gathered, miracles happen. In this moment, my consciousness and yours are connecting; we're meeting in the energetic realm that is the source of all creation, the unmanifest plane where thoughts emerge to come into being. Through the law of three, two hearts coming together leads to an alchemical process in which something new is created. When we interrupt our habitual patterns of perception by inviting in the wisdom of another being, whether human or more-than-human, we shift our habits of consciousness and create space for a miracle.

The heart-opening experience of grace we encounter daily when we lovingly engage with our dogs, cats, trees, each other, and all of creation helps create a sacred space. This can potentially evolve us into depths of beauty we can't even begin to fathom. We live in a quantum reality in which everything affects everything; right now, something new and amazing is happening. Our energy follows our thoughts, *makia,* and now is the time of power, *manawa;* breathe life into that. Right now, our consciousness is expanding; look up and give thanks for the sky, look down and give thanks for the Earth, witness the living moment at play, and sense the dynamic power surging within this and through you. Do something different every day, and try doing it while smiling. As St. John of the Cross shared, "In order to come to the knowledge you have not, you must go by a way you know not." Explore what it's like to conceive of yourself and life in new ways.

Dream bigger than you've ever known possible, then surrender it all.

The yogic term *shunyata* refers to emptiness, and it speaks to the incredible power of presence in which past perceptions of reality do not limit us, therefore being open and available for something better. We're being invited to empty ourselves. We can open our hearts and give thanks in advance because each moment contains an epiphany; we need only be open to it.

We're shifting in quantum ways, and for that, we can be grateful. We can inhale, exhale, and visualize the most beautiful flow of light within, breathing it out into the world and seeing it expanding in all directions, uplifting the entire Universe in wondrous potentiality.

Our *kuleana*, our sacred mission in this lifetime, is to use our power, privilege, voices, and choices to create change. This is what we're here for; we're all collaborating vibrationally in every moment, and that beauty is magnificent. Right now, I'm smiling with you, mirroring your brilliance, celebrating your magic, and inviting you to the most stunning co-creation we've ever imagined. We're blessed, ready, and here for this. The recipe for success is the best of everything for everyone. Simplify, redirect resources, and open the heart; the definition of success is being inspired.

How are we being asked to expand our consciousness to live in greater harmony and integrity with the living Universe?

Explore how this question might come alive in your awareness as you give it space to evolve into inspiration. The force of love, heralding the new Earth, illuminates new possibilities for living together through symbiosis, cooperation, and compassion. Your brilliance is essential for its realization.

What's our shared intention for this lifetime? I sense that our shared desire is for a world that supports the well-being of all life on Earth and beyond, a Universe of harmony. It's possible, and it's happening; the revolution starts from within. Who are you here to be? Your desires are inviting you to a new way of being alive in the world; they're inspiring you to become a more aligned and creative iteration of yourself. Our shared desire for a more harmonious world is calling us to come into resonance with the new life awaiting us; as we reimagine how we see ourselves and each other, we open to new and expansive possibilities.

How can we evolve our identities from within to match our desire for a just world?

We can drop the outworn story of over-consumerism as an acceptable way to live, releasing the thinking that happiness is just over the next horizon or in getting the next thing. We can alchemize late-stage capitalism into a culture of conscious creation in which every choice we make is in the interest of the next seven generations.

An old way is dissolving. Where we direct our attention is where the energy will flow to build the new; it's accelerating, and we're more powerful than we know. Right now, we can take a deep breath and focus our hearts on the vision of a peaceful world where all beings have clean air, water, and food and are well-cared for from birth to the beyond. It's all a practice to learn, develop, evolve, and grow, and the opportunity we're being given is vast and magnificent.

To say "Yes" is to enter into a new way of being, one rooted in the ancient wisdom of our ancestors and illuminated by the new light streaming in from the heartbeat of the Universe.

Offer love and appreciation to the world, and watch it be mirrored back; the vibrational charge of feelings of love and gratitude fuel the new paradigm we're here to birth. We're stoking the fire of creative awakening every time we choose to attune in this way, and soon, all of life becomes a spiritual practice. In fact, it already is—we just sometimes forget. As we practice this awareness of spirit in all creation, our very presence becomes a divinizing power, uplifting and blessing all that we come into connection with as we embody our divinity so that each moment we come into contact with is better because of it, and we are, too.

It's a cellular shift, and we're becoming superhuman, stepping into being more than we've ever known it was possible to be. We can support and nurture this potential in every decision we make by redirecting our privilege toward creating justice, making choices that support Earth-caring companies and humane practices, embodying kindness, and choosing to live more simply and gently on the planet. Every choice we make creates a ripple and affects the entire world, and even a single step in the direction of sustainability contributes to the wave of grace carrying us forward. We're exploring an expansion of our potential; trees aren't limiting who they can become, and every day, they're welcoming in the new intelligence from the Sun, photosynthesizing it into new vibrations of nourishment for their evolution and that of the world. When we open ourselves to the new energies and inspiration coming in, we begin to transform the morphogenetic fields that have been holding our consciousness in place, and we start co-creating a new reality.

Allow yourself to be led, inspired, and surrender any outworn limiting beliefs about how to be alive and who you—and we—can become.

Talk to the plants and stars and share your love with them; allow your beloved canine, equine, and feline companions to open your heart even more fully, transforming you from the inside out; and witness the expansion of harmony all over the Earth and within every aspect of your life. Remember that every breath is an invitation to *Ishvara Pranidhana*, being in continual conversation with the divine, in which you are consciously receiving the grace of being alive as a gateway to perceiving the divinity in all. We came here for this, and I believe in us with all of my heart.

Rumi is sitting beside me as I write, her bright eyes shining with the light of the Universe, her soft breath affirming the magnificence of our aliveness and the miracle of our coexistence in this profound time of awakening and remembrance. Together, we bow in awe to the wild grace connecting our hearts to yours in this living moment. May all beings receive the blessing of this holy now, and may all beings be in love, always and in all ways.

Invitation

Soul Nourishment

Give yourself the best hug, love yourself and all of life wholeheartedly, and feel my eternal gratitude for going on this holy journey with me.
Namaste.

LOVE REVOLUTION PRACTICES

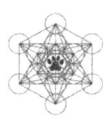

- Educate yourself on racism, sexism, homophobia, ageism, ableism, classism, speciesism, and any other cultural constructs of oppression that you might be contributing to or benefiting from, and make new choices that will support a world of justice for all beings.
- Avoid companies and systems that exploit the more-than-human world, like horse racing, inhumane agriculture or farming, and any of the many other industries profiting from animal abuse.
- Choose local, humane, and regeneratively grown food whenever possible, and support companies devoted to creating food justice.
- Purchase items in sustainable packaging, avoiding single-use plastics and other energy-intensive packaging.
- Support shelters, not breeders.
- Bless the waters.
- Connect and cocreate with the natural world through making offerings to your favorite stones and plants, crafting smudge bundles, full-Moon elixirs, or herbal Sun teas, and engaging in any other acts of kindness that inspire intimacy and collaboration with our more-than-human kindred.
- Love yourself and all of life more and more every day.
- Attune with the cosmos through connecting your heart with the Sun, Moon, stars, and planets.

- Plant gardens, get to know your neighbors, live as organically as possible, share, practice loving kindness to yourself and all others, and remember the power you possess to create justice with every thought you engage and every action you take.
- Breathe, give thanks, and believe in the good things coming. Aloha kea kua.

ACKNOWLEDGMENTS

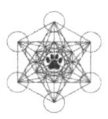

Thank you to my mother, Kay, for being my biggest champion in life and for steadfastly encouraging the birthing of this book; to my father, Jack, and my sisters, Alison and Melissa, for being with me from the very beginning; to my grandfather, Irvin, whose angelic presence has been a source of continual support along the creative journey; to Alix, for her editorial prowess and phenomenal friendship; to Angelyn, for her eternal cheerleading and daily laughter; to Liesl, for her steady presence and joyous accountability; to Lynn, for her spiritual kinship and inspiration; to my nieces and nephew, Daphne, Clara, Zoe, and Matthew, for always being up to play outside, climb trees, and adventure in the woods with me; to Amy and Renee, for inviting me to live in our woodland paradise with them; and most especially to Rumi, my sweetest love, for delightfully interrupting many hours of writing to lure me into play breaks, snuggles, and infinite laughter and joy throughout it all. Lastly, I want to thank this gorgeous living Universe and the sacred forest we call home for holding us in its loving embrace every breath of the way.

ABOUT THE AUTHOR

Holly Clark is an eternal student of the natural realm and a devoted mama to her beloved pup Rumi. Together they delight in learning how to live in harmony with the wild and wonderful world they call home and in inspiring others to join them in creating a just and sustainable existence for all of creation. Holly is a soul companion to fellow travelers on the journey of awakening and remembering and welcomes conscious collaboration with kindred souls.

Learn more at **www.hollyclark.love**

Learn more at **Floweroflifepress.com**

www.ingramcontent.com/pod-product-compliance
Lightning Source LLC
Chambersburg PA
CBHW032045150426
43194CB00006B/431